G000166386

IRELAND 1916–2016

Ireland 1916–2016

The Promise and Challenge of National Sovereignty

Tom Boylan, Nicholas Canny
& Mary Harris

EDITORS

OPEN AIR

Typeset in 11pt on 13.5pt EhrhardtM Pro by
Carrigboy Typesetting Services for OPEN AIR
an imprint of FOUR COURTS PRESS LTD
7 Malpas Street, Dublin 8, Ireland
www.fourcourtspress.ie
and in North America for
FOUR COURTS PRESS
c/o ISBS, 920 NE 58th Avenue, Suite 300, Portland, OR 97213

A catalogue record for this title is available
from the British Library.

ISBN 978-1-84682-681-8

Printed in England,
by CPI Antony Rowe, Chippenham, Wilts.

Contents

Illustrations

Foreword

One of the important ambitions in the planning of the Decade of Centenaries was that in addition to memories of commemorations and celebrations there would be lasting legacies, some in the shape of restoration projects, archives or interpretative centres, but equally important, there would be enduring legacies of an academic and cultural nature.

From the outset, and in particular in the central year of 2016, the academic community rose to the challenge. All of the universities and institutes of higher learning ran their own special programmes often recounting and reflecting on the 1916 experiences of their own staff and students or the experiences of their cities and regions. Lectures and seminars were organized and often focussed on long-forgotten figures, old themes were re-examined in the light of new scholarship. One of the most striking features was the extraordinary engagement of the public with the history and culture of the period helped in no small part by the serious engagement of the media, and in particular RTÉ.

It was against this background that it was decided that there should be one major and overarching national event to draw together the multiple academic, cultural and creative strands. NUI Galway was asked to undertake and make a reality of this project, and under the leadership of Professor Nicholas Canny it did so with great warmth, charm and insight, as well as superb organization and hospitality.

This volume is an elegant record of the proceedings of that conference and reflects great credit on all who made it possible.

Maurice Manning, Chair
Expert Advisory Group
on Commemorations

Brollach

Ar cheann de na huaillmhianta tábhachtacha a bhain le leagan amach Deich mBliana na gCuimhneachán ba ea go mbeadh cuimhní nua á gcruthú chomh maith le bheith ag breathnú siar agus ag comóradh. Ar na cuimhní nua sin bheadh tionscadail athchóirithe, cartlanna nó ionaid léirithe ach chomh tábhachtach céanna bheadh an oidhreacht bhuan acadúil agus chultúrtha.

Ón tús agus go háirithe sa bhliain thábhachtach 2016 thug an pobal acadúil faoin dúshlán go fonnmhar. D'eagraigh gach ollscoil agus institiúid ardléinn a gcláir speisialta féin, ag féachaint siar ar an eolas a bhí ag a bhfoireann agus ag a mic léinn féin ar 1916 nó ar thaithí a gcathracha agus a réigiún ar an tréimhse. Eagraíodh léachtaí agus seimineáir agus dhírigh siad go minic ar dhaoine mór le rá a bhí ligthe i ndearmad, rinneadh athscrúdú ar sheantéamaí i gcomhthéacs léann nua. Bhí an tsuim mhór a chuir an pobal i stair agus i gcultúr na tréimhse ar cheann den na gnéithe ba shuntasaí den chomóradh. Ba chabhair mhór é an spéis ar leith a léirigh na meáin san ábhar, go háirithe RTÉ.

I bhfianaise an mhéid seo glacadh an cinneadh gur cheart go mbeadh ócáid mhór náisiúnta amháin ar siúl chun sraitheanna éagsúla acadúla, cultúrtha agus cruthaitheacha a thabhairt le chéile. Iarradh ar Ollscoil na hÉireann, Gaillimh tabhairt faoin togra seo agus rinne sí é sin le díograis, gnaíúlacht, tuiscint, cóir agus eagar den scoth faoi cheannaireacht an Ollaimh Nicholas Canny.

Taifead snasta é an t-imleabhar seo ar imeachtaí na comhdhála sin agus is léiriú é ar an obair ollmhór a rinne gach duine a bhí páirteach.

Maurice Manning, Cathaoirleach
ar an Sainghrúpa Comhairleach
ar Chuimhneacháin

Preface

NUI Galway was chosen to host an important international academic conference entitled 'Ireland 1916–2016: the promise and challenge of national sovereignty' in November 2016. The conference was intended as the Irish higher-education sector's contribution to a year of reflection on Ireland's nationhood and identity.

Over three days, leading scholars addressed national sovereignty and questioned how the Irish State has delivered on the aspirations of Easter 1916. Deliberations and discussion centred on what the future might hold for Ireland, as a small nation state on the periphery of Europe, in an increasingly globalized future.

Opened on the eve of Remembrance Day (11 November) this conference looked at how Ireland has remembered 1916 and the deep complexity of events in Ireland and Europe in that pivotal year; and examined the various 'promises' made to different strands of Irish society in 1916 and the varying ways in which these were kept.

NUI Galway was pleased to host this important national conversation. The steering group, led by Dr Maurice Manning and Professor Nicholas Canny, took care to ensure wide representation from all elements of higher education on the island of Ireland, with universities, institutes of technology, other colleges, independent scholars and cultural institutions all contributing to a stimulating and enriching conference.

In order to ensure the widest possible access to the conference proceedings, NUI Galway is delighted to publish the plenary papers in this volume. In addition, video of all plenary sessions, featuring introductory comments by each chair and followed by panel discussion, along with opening remarks by the then Taoiseach Enda Kenny TD and others, is available at www.nuigalway.ie/1916.

I would like to commend all those involved in bringing both the conference and this volume to fruition, particularly the plenary speakers, chairs and panel members; the conference steering group; the Department of Education and Skills; the Department of Arts, Heritage and the Gaeltacht; the Ireland 2016 team, the Office of Public Works; and colleagues at NUI Galway.

Jim Browne, President, NUI Galway

Réamhrá

Roghnaíodh OÉ Gaillimh chun comhdháil acadúil idirnáisiúnta tábhachtach a reáchtáil dar teideal, *Éire 1916–2016: Dóchas agus Dúshlán na Ceannasachta Náisiúnta* i mí na Samhna 2016. Ba í aidhm na comhdhála léiriú a thabhairt ar an ionchur a bhí ag earnáil ardoideachais na hÉireann i mbliain inar tugadh náisiúntacht agus féiniúlacht na hÉireann chun cuimhne.

In imeacht trí lá, thug scoláirí mór le rá aghaidh ar cheannasacht náisiúnta agus rinne siad scrúdú ar an gcaoi a bhfuil Stát na hÉireann ag comhlíonadh mhianta na Cásca 1916. Dhírigh an plé agus an díospóireacht ar thodhchaí na hÉireann mar stát beag ar imeall na hEorpa agus muid ag feidhmiú níos mó ar leibhéal domhanda anois ná mar a bhí riamh.

Osclaíodh an chomhdháil an lá roimh Lá an Chuimhneacháin (11 Samhain) agus breathnaíodh ar an gcaoi ar coinníodh 1916 i gcuimhne na ndaoine in Éirinn agus ar chastacht dhomhain na n-imeachtaí in Éirinn agus san Eoraip an bhliain chinniúnach sin; scrúdaíodh na rudaí ar leith a gealladh do ghrúpaí éagsúla i sochaí na hÉireann in 1916 agus na bealaí éagsúla inar comhlíonadh an méid a bhí geallta.

Ba chúis áthais dúinn anseo in OÉ Gaillimh an comhrá náisiúnta tábhachtach seo a reáchtáil. Chinntigh an Grúpa Stiúrtha, faoi cheannas an Dr Maurice Manning agus an Ollaimh Nicholas Canny, go ndearnadh ionadaíocht leathan ar gach gné den ardoideachas ar oileán na hÉireann. Le cabhair ó ollscoileanna, institiúidí teicneolaíochta, coláistí eile, scoláirí neamhspleácha agus institiúidí cultúrtha b'ócáid spreagúil a bhí sa chomhdháil.

D'fhonn go mbeadh teacht ag an oiread daoine agus ab fhéidir ar imeachtaí na comhdhála, tá an-áthas ar OÉ Gaillimh na páipéir iomlánacha a fhoilsiú san imleabhar seo. Ina theannta sin, is féidir teacht ar fhíseáin de na seisiúin iomlánacha, ina bhfuil ráitis tosaigh na gCathaoirleach agus an díospóireacht phainéil, an óráid tosaigh a thug Taoiseach na linne, Enda Kenny TD, agus neart eile ach cuairt a thabhairt ar an láithreán gréasáin www.nuigalway.ie/1916.

Molaim gach duine a bhí páirteach i reáchtáil na comhdhála agus i gcur le chéile an imleabhair seo, go háirithe na Cainteoirí, na Cathaoirligh agus baill na bPainéal; Grúpa Stiúrtha na Comhdhála; an Roinn Oideachais agus Scileanna agus an Roinn Ealaíon, Oidhreachta agus Gaeltachta; chomh maith le Foireann Éire 2016, Oifig na nOibreacha Poiblí agus comhghleacaithe in OÉ Gaillimh.

Jim Browne, Uachtarán, OÉ Gaillimh

Acknowledgments

This volume of plenary papers is based on the successful conference, 'Ireland 1916–2016: the promise and challenge of national sovereignty', which was held at NUI Galway from 10–12 November 2016.

The organization of the conference was led by a steering group chaired by Dr Maurice Manning, with academic direction by Professor Nicholas Canny – with the support of the president of Ireland, Michael D. Higgins – and comprised of members John Concannon, Orlaith Lochrin and Michael O'Reilly of the Ireland 2016 centenary programme office; Professor Tom Boylan, Dr Jim Browne, Dr Mary Harris, Sandra Glennon, Caroline Loughnane and Liz McConnell of NUI Galway; Professor Mary Daly, Royal Irish Academy; Christy Mannion, Department of Education and Skills; and Dr Jim Murray, Institutes of Technology Ireland.

From the outset there was great interest among the Irish academic community in this conference and its subject matter. Plenary speakers and panellists accepted the invitation to participate with enthusiasm and the success of the conference was principally due to the calibre of these participants, which included the following introductory speakers, chairs, plenary speakers and panellists (in order): Dr Jim Browne, president, NUI Galway; Seán Ó Foghlú, secretary general, Department of Education and Skills; Professor Nicholas Canny, NUI Galway; Professor Philip Pettit, Princeton University; Professor Iseult Honohan, UCD; An Taoiseach Enda Kenny TD; Professor Mary Daly, RIA; Professor Roy Foster, Oxford University; Professor Anne Dolan, TCD; Professor Anthony McElligott, University of Limerick; Dr Ríona Ní Fhrighil, NUI Galway; Professor Emmet O'Connor, University of Ulster; Professor Graham Walker, Queen's University Belfast; Heather Humphreys TD, minister for arts, heritage, regional, rural and Gaeltacht affairs; John Concannon, Ireland 2016 centenary programme office; Fintan O'Toole, *Irish Times*; Professor Clair Wills, Princeton University; Professor Claire Connolly, UCC; Louise Lowe, ANU Productions; John McAuliffe, University of Manchester; Professor John McHale, NUI Galway; Professor Kevin Hjortshøj O'Rourke, Oxford University; Professor Alan Barrett, ESRI; Professor Mary Corcoran, Maynooth University; Anthony Foley, DCU; Professor Eoin O'Leary, UCC; Dr Conor Skehan, Dublin Institute of Technology; Dr Mary Canning, HEA; Professor Louise Richardson, Oxford University; Professor Dympna

Devine, UCD; Professor Willie Donnelly, Waterford Institute of Technology; Dr Niamh Hourigan, UCC; Professor Fionnuala Waldron, DCU; Dr Maurice Manning, NUI; Professor Brendan O'Leary, University of Pennsylvania; Dr Niall Ó Dochartaigh, NUI Galway; Professor Jennifer Todd, UCD; Dee Forbes, RTÉ; James Hickey, Irish Film Board; Professor Patrick Lonergan, NUI Galway; Mary McCarthy, Culture Ireland; and Aideen Howard, The Ark.

Funding and support for the academic conference was provided by the Department of Education and Skills, the Department of Arts, Heritage, Regional, Rural and Gaeltacht Affairs (through the Ireland 2016 centenary programme office) and National University of Ireland, Galway. Operational support was provided by Patricia Walsh, NUI Galway conference office, along with Ireland 2016 centenary programme's Madeline Boughton, Medbh Killilea, Neil Carron, and colleagues from the Office of Public Works.

The publication of this volume is part of NUI Galway's programme to mark Ireland's Decade of Centenaries, entitled, 'A nation rising | Éire á múscailt'. Led by Dr Mary Harris during 2016, this programme comprised of fourteen academic conferences, numerous seminars, lectures and artistic and public events; the establishment of the post of 1916 scholar in residence; and a special exhibition, 'A university in war and revolution, 1913–1919: the University College Galway experience'.

Abbreviations

BMH	Bureau of Military History
DUP	Democratic Unionist Party
ECHR	European Convention on Human Rights
EEC	European Economic Community
EFTA	European Free Trade Association
ERP	Ejército Revolucionario del Pueblo (People's Revolutionary Army)
FARC	Fuerzas Armadas Revolucionarias de Colombia (Revolutionary Armed Forces of Colombia)
FDI	foreign direct investment
GDP	gross domestic product
GFA	Good Friday Agreement
GNP	gross national product
IDA	Industrial Development Authority
LSE	London School of Economics
MNCs	multinational corporations
NATO	North Atlantic Treaty Organization
NUI	National University of Ireland
NUIG	National University of Ireland, Galway
OECD	Organization for Economic Co-operation and Development
OEEC	Organization for European Economic Co-operation
PKK	Partiya Karkerên Kurdistan – Kurdistan Workers' Party
PSNI	Police Service of Northern Ireland
RIA	Royal Irish Academy
SDLP	Social Democratic and Labour Party
SF	Sinn Féin
TCD	Trinity College Dublin
UCC	University College Cork
UCD	University College Dublin
UCL	University College London
UDA	Ulster Defence Association
UUP	Ulster Unionist Party
UVF	Ulster Volunteer Force

Introduction

Tom Boylan, Nicholas Canny
and Mary Harris

This conference volume includes the six plenary addresses (some in revised form) given at the conference entitled 'Ireland 1916–2016: the promise and challenge of national sovereignty' that convened at the National University of Ireland, Galway from 10–12 November 2016. This conference, held on behalf of all third-level institutions in Ireland, was the concluding 2016 contribution of the third-level educational sector in Ireland to the commemoration of the Easter Rising of 1916, with input from the government's Expert Advisory Group on Commemorations, Ireland 1916, the Department of Education and Skills, the Institutes of Technology Ireland and the Royal Irish Academy. It was supported financially by the Department of Education and Skills, for which the organizers are very grateful.

Since this was the principal collective contribution of the third-level institutions to the commemoration of 1916, an informing principle was the need to facilitate the widest possible participation from universities in Ireland, both North and South, along with the Irish institutes of technology. Consequently, the chairs of the various sessions and the respondents to the plenary speakers were selected to ensure participation across the third-level sector on the island of Ireland. A unique feature of the conference was the decision by the organizers that the plenary speakers should be drawn from academics of Irish birth or origin who hold senior positions in some of the world's leading universities. This was to acknowledge the achievements of the Irish diaspora in the realm of ideas and to furnish this distinguished group of invited scholars with the opportunity to reflect on events in Ireland over the last century. It was also considered that speakers based outside of Ireland were more likely to reflect trans-nationally on the events of 1916 and what flowed from them.

The brief of the speakers, chairs and respondents was to encourage the audience, and the readers of this colloquium volume, to consider how the generations of Irish people who have succeeded the women and men involved with the Easter Rising in 1916 have responded to that event, and how Irish people of the present generation are using, and can use, the national sovereignty that has been gifted to them by their predecessors to improve the condition of humanity at home and universally. The six revised plenary addresses that are published here show that each of the invited speakers responded valiantly to this challenge, even if they would be the first to acknowledge that their views have been sharpened by the interventions of the chairs and commentators and by the lively discussions that followed each session. The topics selected for discussion were the outcome of negotiations between the speakers and the organizers of the conference conducted with the purpose of addressing a selective number of broad thematic areas, including historical contextualization and reassessment, and current and likely future concerns and challenges confronting Irish people and an independent Irish state.

Philip Pettit's paper, 'European republicanism: the past and the potential', traces the trajectory of republican political philosophy from its origins in Rome, with its attendant principle of freedom as non-domination and a theory of government based on the principle of a mixed constitution. This excursus shows how these principles developed over time into the philosophy of classical republicanism and made their way through medieval and early modern Europe. These ideas proved remarkably durable, and Pettit explains how they exerted significant influence over both the victors in the American war of independence and the participants in the French Revolution. He shows how, by the late eighteenth century, classical republicanism had run into its philosophical nemesis, classical liberalism, with its subtle but powerful shifts, particularly in its view of freedom from non-domination to non-coercion, and from concerns with the freedom of persons to the freedom of choice. Pettit moves from classical republicanism and classical liberalism to their offspring, neo-republicanism and neo-liberalism, and makes a measured but insistent case in favour of neo-republicanism as the desired way forward.

Ireland merits mention in Pettit's paper thanks to the rising of the United Irishmen in 1798 and the writings of Wolfe Tone, who was committed to the doctrine of classical republicanism. This is relevant to the theme of this volume because Irish republicans of future generations would draw inspiration from the republican principles advocated by Tone. Successive authors in this collection find, however, that Irish republicanism tended to utilize this inherited tradition primarily to mobilize support for national independence, and more specifically for the military means to achieve separation from Britain, which, to a degree, was realized by the Irish Free State that was established following the Anglo-Irish Treaty of 1922. Several of our authors show how the influence of a narrowly focused cultural nationalism and a hegemonic institutional Catholic church shaped and distorted the wider republican tradition in Irish circumstances over the first four to five decades of independence. Pettit's paper, which is an expansion and revision of his conference presentation, provides an impressive intellectual contextualization to the contributions that follow.

While Roy Foster in his paper takes account of the contraction of the broader republican philosophy and political agenda that justified the Rising of 1916 and the political independence that followed some years later, he highlights the cacophony of voices that were to be heard during the years of revolution, 1912–23, arguing always that events in Ireland were part of 'a wider dislocation' that was 'decisively shaped by the Great War, indeed as a theatre of that war'. Building on his own recent work on this revolutionary period, Foster argues that 'early twentieth-century Ireland saw a period of destabilization in all sorts of areas', including labour relations, religion, gender relations, and the family, in addition to the dynamics of nationalist politics. But he argues that soon after the events of 1916 the rhetoric of radical nationalism gained the dominant position in the public discourse and succeeded in dislodging 'those other rhetorics', which included secularist, feminist, social-democratic and socialist tropes. He shows how, under these circumstances, many promises withered on the vine as independent Ireland during its first half-century of existence settled into being a deeply conservative, culturally constricted and socially deprived society. This outcome disappointed many who had been associated with the Revolution primarily because it failed what Philip Pettit describes as 'the eye ball test', by which he means the creation of a political climate where adult people, regardless of gender, rank, race or economic circumstance may 'look one another in the eye without reason for fear or favour'. On a more positive note, Foster's survey charts the emergence in the second fifty years of independence of the slow and painful progression towards a more open and more equitable society, although this arguably still falls short of Pettit's neo-republican ideal.

Negotiating the relationship between culture and globalization, and more specifically the 'challenges for Irish art and culture in an era of globalization' and the 'ways in which the current era might differ from, and respond to previous "world" moments in the history of Irish literature and culture', is the focus of Clair Wills' presentation to the conference. Wills engages a number of substantive issues, including the primacy of the ethnographic method, the efficacy of site-specific works of art, and the dynamic interaction between memory in 'historical space' and in 'performance space', all of which 'asks us to reflect on the nature of historical knowledge'. She skilfully invokes James Joyce's work, and more particularly the fact that if 1916 was a pivotal act for the future foundation of the Irish state, it was also the year that saw the publication of *A portrait of the artist as a young man*, a seminal act in the foundation of a 'literature which would interrogate that state'. But, more pointedly, she identifies in Joyce's *Ulysses*, which he was writing during the course of 1916, three challenges to the national story, namely the 'question of history', the issue of the 'boundaries of national identity', and the 'search for maturity for a new and better family'.

Within the conceptual framework provided by the challenges she identified in Joyce, Wills skilfully analyses a number of contemporary Irish writers and their recent work, including Seamus Deane, Colm Tóibín, Anne Enright, Emma Donoghue and Kevin Barry. She identifies the complexity for instance of 'generational conflict' and its continuing influence in shaping 'a great deal of contemporary fiction and drama', which she views as 'one of the legacies of 1916'. But she contends also that the 'mirror image' of generational conflict is 'generational haunting', or the idea of an incomplete past – 'a past that because of its incompleteness keeps intruding into the present'. Fiction and drama may always be a more effective mode of exploring the hidden histories of familial activities, for instance physical and sexual abuse, and by analogy the concealed collusion between church and state in maintaining horrific institutional regimes. Wills certainly thinks so. But of all the modes of artistic creation, she is insistent that the ethnographic method, or 'impulse' as she terms it, has proved the most productive for a variety of contemporary cultural practices that seek to interrogate 'the stories the nation tells itself'. She finds that ethnography as a methodology and set of procedures is the motive force for much of the most compelling contemporary work, with intriguing implications for the 'nature of historical knowledge'. Wills argues that artworks based on the ethnographic method offer an alternative to 'broader national histories' by focusing on local memory, and the exploration of particular landscapes and social environments that are 'saturated with shared associations'. In keeping with her commitment to think about the different ways in which cultural practices challenge the 'stories' a nation wishes to convey to itself as part of its self-conscious narrative, she believes we will need the ethnographers, interpreters and translators of these 'stories', or more specifically the novelists, poets, film-makers, composers, dramatists and artists, to discern and reveal their omitted, suppressed and hidden elements. In this respect she concludes that contemporary Irish society, no less than Irish society in the past, has been well served by its writers and artists.

Kevin Hjortshøj O'Rourke addresses independent Ireland's economic performance, and in doing so shows that in this domain the rhetoric of the 'promises' of sovereignty, the reality of the achievements delivered and the 'challenges' of the future are exposed to measurable evaluation as well as to conceptual interrogation. In contrast to the complexities of national identity, cultural uniqueness and identity politics that concern other authors, O'Rourke shows that the economic narrative is informed by an altogether more pragmatic set of considerations given the realities of the small, open and highly dependent economy that necessarily prevailed in independent Ireland. For the newly emergent Irish state, the issues of economic survival, sustained capacity building and long-term development proved to be the major issues that needed to be addressed. O'Rourke shows how these became reliant upon the economic strategies pursued and their ensuing outcomes, all within the parameters of changing domestic and external environments. The most striking feature of O'Rourke's paper is that it reassesses Ireland's economic performance over the twentieth century within an extended comparative analytical framework.

For anyone still subscribing to the notion of 'Irish exceptionalism', O'Rourke's paper will provide a rude awakening, since his comparative analysis leads to the conclusions that: 1) the economic history of independent Ireland was not particularly unusual; 2) Ireland's linkages to the UK economy led to an over-dependence on what was one of the poorest performing economies in Europe for much of the twentieth century; and 3) Ireland's eventual membership of the European Economic Community (EEC) in 1973, and later its integration into the single market, proved 'crucial'. Along the way O'Rourke provides a number of interesting conclusions concerning particular issues, such as protectionism in the inter-war period, Ireland's neutrality during the Second World War, and Ireland's default on the land annuities payable to Britain that led to the economic war.

While he points to some fortunate economic decisions made by Irish political leaders during the 1930s and 1940s, O'Rourke also identifies some mistakes and serious failures of policy in the post-1950 period, particularly the delayed liberalization of the Irish economy, especially in the domain of trade policy. This leads to his conclusion that the funereal litany of unemployment, economic stagnation, low incomes and massive population loss through emigration prompts one to ask if Ireland was not stricken by a 'national death wish'. He finds that at this time even sovereignty appeared fragile and the promises of the revolutionary generation sounded increasingly hollow. However, he concludes that salvation came from the intellectual and political leadership of the Whitaker–Lemass partnership combined with major external developments such as the establishment of the EEC.

While O'Rourke takes account of some dissenting voices concerning Ireland's decision to join the EEC, he contends that Irish sovereignty and EU membership have complemented rather than come into conflict with each other. This appraisal leads to his consideration of Ireland's likely future relationships with a UK that is at the point of withdrawing from membership of the European Union, with a European economy that will certainly be reconfigured in the aftermath of a UK withdrawal, and with a US that seems to be becoming increasingly isolationist in its economic policy. He contends that survival, albeit at a very different level compared with 1922 or the 1950s, rather than sovereignty is likely to become Ireland's dominant concern for the foreseeable future.

Louise Richardson, who is a leading scholar in the field of international security and terrorist activity as well as being the vice chancellor of the University of Oxford, considers the 'role of education' or more specifically the role of universities, 'in addressing the challenges of the twenty-first century'. She identifies a number of major challenges facing the university sector, no less in Ireland than throughout the world, but confines herself to two such challenges in particular: the relationship between university education and political violence, and the role of universities in redressing societal inequality. Her conclusion with respect to the issue of political violence is less than comforting in current circumstances, in that while universities 'do not cause radicalization ... nor has university education prevented individuals from becoming terrorists'. On the second issue, societal inequality, Richardson believes that in the future there is likely to be a 'direct correlation' between the capacity of universities to educate 'a broader section of society and the degree of social instability experienced by these societies'.

At the heart of Richardson's position is a serious interrogation of the quality and relative emphasis of what is offered in current university education. This is centred on the dilemma that if universities increasingly focus on training a skilled workforce, as they are frequently expected to do by official policy in many countries, they are likely to 'lose the opportunity to provide an education that is so much broader and more important'. For Richardson, in relation to her analysis of political violence and university education, a commitment to a university education that produces a generation imbued with the values of 'thinking critically, acting ethically, and always questioning' both the official ideologies of governments and ideologies in general, is now of paramount importance to the achievement of social stability within a civilized society. She believes that it should also be a system of education that 'teaches empathy to others, that exposes its students to a cosmopolitan community of scholars that delights in difference rather than fears it, and that inculcates the belief that truth is an aspiration not a possession'. These fundamental values of education restated by Richardson pose very fundamental and challenging questions with respect to the balance and content of our university education. The responsibility of universities in the twenty-first century, arising from Richardson's analysis, namely to educate present and future generations in ethical and moral sensitivities, in empathy, tolerance and openness to difference, is a formidable and challenging one when faced with competing if not conflicting demands from government and society. She recognizes that this challenge has particular relevance to the commemoration of the 1916 Rising because Patrick Pearse and those of his associates who were connected with St Enda's – the school that Pearse had established in 1908 – 'cared passionately about education' and identified with the most advanced 'child-centred' educational programmes of their day, which they hoped would displace the murderously utilitarian education favoured by the state and society they aspired and conspired to overthrow.

Where the presentation by Louise Richardson, one of the world's most influential university leaders of today, challenges readers to think about how Ireland (or at least Ireland's university sector) might make a global contribution to improving the human condition, that of Brendan O'Leary, a distinguished political scientist, explains how dramatic changes that are external to Ireland, and over which Irish people exert little control, challenge the continued existence of an Irish state, and more immediately, the relatively harmonious relationships that currently obtain between the Republic of Ireland and Northern Ireland and also between the various communities within Northern Ireland. The first global issue to which O'Leary gives brief, terrifying consideration is climate change, but most of his paper is devoted to BREXIT (or UKEXIT, as he would have it) and its implications for the future of Ireland. He outlines ten possible outcomes for Ireland (some positive and most negative), and he arrives at a fairly optimistic prediction that Ireland has a reasonable prospect of surviving as an independent nation state within the framework of the European Union, and that it may even become a protector and negotiator for Northern Ireland in Brussels, with the tacit agreement of a UK government.

* * *

The essays in this volume provide an outstanding overview of the emergence, survival and achievements of Irish sovereignty from its troubled origins in the early twentieth century. For those commentators in Ireland who expressed apprehension concerning the shaping of the centenary commemoration of 1916 due to the complexities associated with memory reconstruction and representation, their fears have been allayed by the events that unfolded over 2016, which is a tribute to the organizers of the centenary commemorations. The scale, scope and coverage of what proved to be an extraordinarily extensive programme ensured a unique level of inclusivity, participation by the general public, while attention was also given in a measured and dignified manner to the military dimension to the 1916 Rising. The nuanced and extended frameworks that informed and shaped the 2016 centenary commemoration were in no small part due to the impressive and extended research of Irish scholars at home and abroad, including the contributors to this volume, over the last thirty years and more. While proclamation of ideals in 1916 is not to be equated with delivery in 2016, the Irish nation state stands more assured in its sovereignty today than it has at any stage since independence. The contributions to the Galway conference, and to this volume that has resulted from it, provide a fitting testimony as to why and how this was achieved.

European republicanism: the past and the potential

PHILIP PETTIT

In this paper, I provide a sketch of the European republican view of freedom and government, marking out its appearance and development in Ireland. And then, looking forward, I highlight the potential of this long, shared tradition of thinking for contemporary politics. As a philosophy of government, I argue, neo-republicanism offers a very attractive alternative to the neo-liberalism that has been recently dominant in policy circles.[1]

The paper is in three main sections. In the first, I provide a short history of classic republican thinking in Europe and Ireland. In a second, briefer section, I describe the rise of classical liberalism, which displaced republican thought over the following century. And in the third, I look at the alternatives represented in contemporary thought by neo-republicanism and neo-liberalism, highlighting what I see as the advantages of the neo-republican approach.

THE CLASSICAL REPUBLICAN TRADITION

The republican, Roman idea of freedom

This republican idea of freedom goes back to Rome's republican days, and to the enormously influential writings of figures like Polybius, Cicero and Livy.[2] In this way of thinking about freedom, which was to survive for two

---

1 I rely heavily in this paper on earlier work, including P. Pettit, *Republicanism: a theory of freedom and government* (Oxford, 1997) and P. Pettit, *Just freedom: a moral compass for a complex world* (New York, 2014). I borrow freely from three recent papers: P. Pettit, 'Freedom and the state: nanny or nightwatchman?', *Public Health*, 30 (2015), 1–6; P. Pettit, 'A brief history of liberty – and its lessons', *Journal of Human Development and Capability*, 17 (2016), 5–21; and P. Pettit, 'The tree of liberty: republicanism, American, French and Irish', *Field Day Review*, 1 (2005), 29–41. For an overview of contemporary work on neo-republicanism, see F. Lovett & P. Pettit, 'Neo-republicanism: a normative and institutional research program', *Annual Review of Political Science*, 12 (2009), 18–29. 2 While Greek ideas of freedom had influenced the Roman tradition, they received a degree of emphasis in Roman thinking that was unprecedented and they were linked in an original way with the idea of the republic that Rome embodied and that Polybius in particular celebrated. See V. Arena, *Libertas and the practice of politics in the late Roman*

millennia, to be free meant to be a free person. And to be a free person in turn meant, first, that you did not have to live under the will of a master; and, second, that this wasn't just a matter of good luck: you were adequately resourced and protected against being controlled by a master's will.

How, according to Roman thinking, did you get to be a free person – a *liber* – in this sense? The general assumption was that all citizens – in effect, all non-enslaved, native men – could expect to be equally free, at least in the ideal. And so, the idea was that the citizens of a society would be free insofar as two conditions are satisfied. First, the law defines a range of choices – later, to be called the basic or fundamental liberties – where they are individually able to act as they wish, without being subject to the private will of another. And second, the law that guards them in this way does not itself represent the imposition of a public will by a monarch or any such power: it is framed on terms that the citizens collectively impose on their government.

This conception of what it is to enjoy freedom meant that there were two ways in which you might be un-free. One, by being subject to the private will of another, as in being the slave of a master or a woman subject to her husband's will. Two, by living under a law that is imposed at the will of a particular person or party, not under a law that, together with other citizens, you have a part in shaping. The Latin word for subjection to the will of another – subjection to a master or *dominus* – was *dominatio*, which we may translate as 'domination'.[3] And so the idea was that freedom requires the absence of both private and public domination.

To enjoy freedom as non–domination in your private life, according to this conception, is to be able to choose as you wish in the exercise of what the law designates as the basic liberties. To have that freedom is to be able to say what you think, associate with others for legally permissible purposes, move where you wish within the country, take up any occupation on offer and operate in the market to the extent that your resources allow. Not everyone in Rome had access to such a private realm of free choice: not slaves, of course; not women; indeed, not anyone subject to a domestic master. While only citizens could be free, however, the ideal of being a free citizen would have been cherished by all, even those who could not hope to attain it.

One of the signature themes in the Roman conception of private freedom was the insistence that if you are subject to someone else's domination – if their will is paramount in the area, roughly, of your basic liberties – then that

republic (Cambridge, 2012). And on some Greek connections, see E. Nelson, *The Greek tradition in Republican thought* (Cambridge, 2004) and M. Lane, 'Placing Plato in the history of liberty', *History of European Ideas*, 43 (2017).   3 On this notion see the appendix in F. Lovett, *A general theory of domination and justice* (Oxford, 2010).

makes you un-free, even if the master in your life is entirely good-willed and inclined to let you choose in that area according to your own wishes. Thus, Roman comedies made fun of the figure of the slave who thought he was free because his master was gentle or gullible or just often away.[4]

What ensured your freedom as non-domination in public as distinct from private life? The fact that as a citizen you could play a part in determining the shape of the law under which your basic liberties, and those of your fellow citizens, were defined and protected. While the law interfered in the life of all, its main role was to establish and defend basic liberties. And in serving personal freedom in that way it would not have taken away from your public freedom, provided that it was not dictated by a political master like a king; provided, more positively, that it was enacted under constraints that you and your fellow citizens imposed in a more or less equal distribution of political power.

The Roman distribution of power gave various privileges to the noble, wealthy classes, who could hold public office and, by the same token, have a place in the senate, an essentially executive or administrative council. But there were a variety of constraints that ordinary citizens could impose on those in office and on the laws established. While only officials could propose laws, for example, the laws had to be passed by one of a number of legislative bodies in which all citizens could take part. Moreover, those officials had to gain office by annual election at the hand of the citizenry generally. Again, anything they proposed to do in office could be vetoed by one of the tribunes (officials whose job it was to look after the interests the plebeian, generally poorer sectors of society). And of course, the application of the laws was determined by more or less popular courts, in which up to two hundred people – citizens of a certain rank – could take part.

These arrangements introduced different centres of power that could check and balance one another, with the more senior, consular officials operating like a king, the senate operating like an aristocracy, and the citizenry at large performing as in a democracy. Polybius described this as a mixed constitution, invoking an older Greek idea. It mixed up the way in which power was exercised, making it difficult for anyone to assume the role of the absolute king.

The Romans conceived of their republic as a society in which no one individual could ever be a king (an absolute king, since that is what monarchy would have connoted for them). Indeed, the republic had begun with the

4 See Q. Skinner, *Liberty before liberalism* (Cambridge, 1998), which is a central text in the development of contemporary republican thought, for his discussion of the figure of Tranio in Plautus' play *Mostellaria*.

overthrow of Tarquin, the last king of Rome, late in the sixth century BCE. Those who later followed the Roman, republican way of thinking always maintained that to live under a law that was subject even to a wholly benevolent king was to live in un-freedom. In order to live in freedom the law had to be a public affair – a *res publica* – not something in the control of any private power.

Medieval and early modern Europe

This Roman way of thinking about freedom identified it, then, with the enjoyment of both private and public non-domination: the enjoyment of a status in which you were the equal – the publicly marked equal – of any other citizen. This ideal was never fully realized in republican Rome, of course – the wealthy commanded large groups of dependent clients among their fellow citizens – and, despite continuing lip-service, it became more and more irrelevant with the rise of the empire at the beginning of the millenium. But the ideal regained a powerful presence in public life more than a thousand years later, with the rise of the city-states of northern Italy (Venice, Florence, Siena and Perugia) and the other centres of the high Middle Ages.

The burghers of these new trading centres had generally thrown off the control of local lords by the late twelfth century and began at this point to cast themselves as citizens in the Roman mould. They insisted that living under a law that was of their own collective making, and being each protected in an individual sphere of choice by that law – being secured in their basic liberties – they enjoyed exactly the sort of freedom that the Romans cherished. And since their trading centres became the great centres of learning in the Renaissance period, they bequeathed this neo-Roman way of thinking about freedom to the Northern European countries in the 1500s and 1600s.

The legacy of republican thinking that these northern countries inherited led in many cases to constitutional upheavals. It shaped the republic of the nobles in Poland, it inspired the Dutch republic that was formed after the expulsion of the Spanish, and it fuelled the revolution that led to the English revolution and the republic of the 1640s and 1650s. Thomas Hobbes, an opponent of the English revolution, railed at this 'false show of liberty', remarking famously that 'there was never anything so dearly bought as these western parts have bought the learning of the Greek and Latin tongues'.[5]

The republican conception of freedom that inspired these upheavals remained in common currency in the English-speaking world, even after the

5 T. Hobbes & E. Curley (eds), *Leviathan* (Indianapolis, 1994), chapter 21.

restoration of Charles II in 1660. Indeed, with the introduction of a broadly constitutional monarchy after 1688 – a monarchy that was no longer seen as necessarily inimical to republican freedom – it came to be endorsed as an ideal, albeit differently interpreted, in most strains of political thinking. Freedom in this sense consists in 'independency upon the will of another', as Algernon Sidney put it in the 1680s.[6] Or as the idea was formulated in *Cato's letters*, a radical tract of the 1700s, 'Liberty is, to live upon one's own terms; slavery is, to live at the mere mercy of another.'[7] *Cato's letters* became a recognized statement of the commonwealth-man or radical Whig perspective, as it was known. This was essentially a full-blooded republican perspective, tempered only by an acceptance of a constitutional, restricted version of monarchy.

In the commonwealth-man way of thinking, true to its Roman origins, you were un-free even if your master or lord was entirely good-willed. As Sidney had written, 'he is a slave who serves the best and gentlest man in the world, as well as he who serves the worst'.[8] And that message was taken, not just to outlaw the private domination of a gentle individual master, but also the public domination of a gentle colonial master. Writing in the 1770s, the clergyman and mathematician Richard Price – a radical Whig – emphasized the point forcefully. 'Individuals in private life, while held under the power of masters, cannot be denominated free, however equitably and kindly they may be treated. This is strictly true of communities as well as of individuals.'[9] The observation was central to the case made by American colonists against being ruled, however equitably, by the British government.

America and France

The republican conception of freedom as non-domination reached the point of its influence in the course of that American struggle. One of the things that had really upset the American colonists is that in 1766, when the Westminster parliament had been persuaded to withdraw the tax imposed by the Stamp Act, it went out of its way to claim that, although choosing to exercise indulgence, it enjoyed as 'of right' the 'full power and authority to make laws and statutes' binding the Americans. This was just to say that it claimed the position of a master, albeit a kindly master, giving substance to Price's complaint. If that claim was admitted then, by the received ideal, the American colonists could not count as free. Despite the existence of actual

---

6 A. Sidney, *Discourses concerning government* (Indianapolis, 1990), 17.　　7 J. Trenchard & T. Gordon, *Cato's letters* (New York, 1971), ii, pp 249–50.　　8 *Discourses concerning government*, p. 441.　　9 R. Price, *Political writings* (Cambridge, 1991), pp 77–8.

slaves in the American lands, this led to a general complaint among the colonists, in the words of a 1772 resolution in Boston, that 'we are degraded from the rank of free subjects to the despicable condition of slaves'.[10]

A few years before the American colonists had begun to rebel against British rule, Jean Jacques Rousseau had espoused essentially the received ideal of republican freedom in *The social contract*, published in 1762.[11] And it was his work, more than anyone else's, that shaped the thinking of those who inspired the French Revolution in 1789. Unlike many earlier republicans, Rousseau had a relatively inclusive view of the citizenry – they would be restricted to men but not to propertied, mainstream men – and argued for the importance of an extended form of equal freedom.

For Rousseau, as for other republicans, the un-freedom from which the state should protect citizens equally is, as he suggests in a number of places, 'personal dependence' or 'individual dependence' (1.7.8; 2.11.1), a condition that he also describes as 'servitude' (4.8.28). This is the condition against which he had railed in *The second discourse* of 1755, when he said that 'in the relations between man and man the worst that can happen to one is to find himself at the other's discretion'.[12] Thus the freedom that Rousseau values is clearly a version of freedom as non-domination, requiring in the words of *The social contract* 'that every citizen be perfectly independent of all the others' (2.12.3).[13] He says that what 'ought to be the end of every system of legislation is ... freedom and equality', where equality is valued 'because freedom cannot subsist without it' (2.11.1).

While both the American and French revolutions were inspired by republican ideals, however, they divided on one crucial matter. The Americans continued to remain faithful to the ideal of the mixed constitution and the checks and balances it would introduce; this fidelity is marked to this day in the constitution, introduced in 1787, which takes the idea of mixture to the extreme of allowing frequent gridlock.

Following Rousseau, however, the French tended to think that the best guarantor of public freedom – the best guarantor against allowing one

---

10 J.P. Reid, *The concept of liberty in the age of the American Revolution* (Chicago, 1988), p. 92.   11 V. Gourevitch (ed.), *Rousseau: the social contract and other later political writings* (Cambridge, 1997).   12 V. Gourevitch (ed.), *Rousseau: the discourses and other early political writings* (Cambridge, 1997), p. 176. The dependence mentioned here is not that which living with others inescapably entails, only dependence involving domination: subjection to another's will. Rousseau emphasizes in a letter of 1757 that he has nothing against the inescapable form of dependence, acknowledging that 'everything is to one degree or another subject to this universal dependency'. See J. Starobinski, 'A letter from Jean-Jacques Rousseau (1757)', *New York Review of Books* (New York, 2003), 31–2. 13 See J.F. Spitz, *La liberté politique* (Paris, 1995).

individual or elite to control the law – is to have a central, unified assembly of all, giving it sovereignty over each, considered as an individual. Where Italian-Atlantic republicans had wanted a law controlled by no central will, but answerable to the citizenry as a whole, the French republicans looked for an arrangement under which there would be a controlling will: the general will of the people, expressed in majority voting within an assembly of citizens.

Ireland

With full access to the English-speaking world, Ireland was as much a home to commonwealth or radical Whig ideas as America. These ideas circulated particularly in dissenter circles. This is unsurprising, since Presbyterians and other dissenting groups were generally literate; were denied political and other rights, like Catholics; and had many family and other connections with those who took part in the American war of independence. Fearing that dissenters would revolt against Westminster's rule, as their cousins had in the American colonies, the Westminster parliament gave them political rights in 1782 and allowed them to be represented in the Dublin parliament.

Perhaps the most striking testament to the presence of commonwealth-man or republican ideas in Ireland at this time is the stance that the Dublin parliament took to the repeal in 1782 of Poynings' Law. Introduced in 1494, that law had the effect of allowing measures passed in Dublin to come into effect only if the Westminster parliament agreed, and the repeal of that law was undoubtedly meant to keep the Irish happy and avoid a repeat of the American Revolution. The motivation may have been very similar to the motivation behind the repeal of the Stamp Act in 1766.

But many in the Dublin parliament responded to the repeal of Poynings' Law in much the same way that many American colonists had responded to the repeal of the Stamp Act.[14] Led by Henry Flood, they campaigned for a renunciation of the law by the Westminster parliament, not merely its repeal. The argument was that repealing the law was consistent with claiming a power to reinstate it at will; and that it suggested therefore that the Irish parliament was subject to the power of its British counterpart, even if that power in at least this instance was exercised in an equitable and kindly manner, to recall Price's words.

The 1782 constitution, and 'Grattan's parliament' of the 1780s and 1790s, proved to be a great disappointment for the radical Whigs in Ireland, among

14 A.T.Q. Stewart, *A deeper silence: the hidden roots of the United Irish movement* (London, 1993), pp 41–3.

them Theobald Wolfe Tone, who had penned pamphlets as 'A Radical Whig' and 'A Northern Whig'. The business of the parliament was effectively manipulated by Dublin Castle, with the lord lieutenant having a far more effective degree of control over who would rule there than the king had in relation to the Westminster parliament. It was despair over the prospects for ever realizing republican ideals through the Dublin parliament that led Wolfe Tone and others to establish the United Irishmen in 1791, and ultimately to seek full independence for Ireland. As Tone said in commentary on that parliament. 'We are free in theory, we are slaves in fact.'[15]

The United Irishmen embraced the rhetoric of independence and freedom with a fervour equal to that of the Americans or the French, as indeed this language of slavery suggests. The sentiment is well expressed in the Bantry Bay declaration of 1796: 'True republicans fight only to vindicate the rights of equality and detest ever the name of a master.'[16] Writing from America, after fleeing there in the 1790s, Tone gave expression to the core idea when he said that he could never live in a country where he had to depend on the leave or permission of others. 'I would exist in no country *permissu superiorum.*'[17] To live under a master, private or public, would inevitably involve depending on his grace and favour – effectively, his permission – for being able to act at will, even within the range of the basic liberties.

THE CLASSICAL LIBERAL TRADITION

An alternative conception of freedom

And now we confront one of the great ironies in the history of political thought. At just the time when the republican conception of freedom attained its greatest influence, sparking a successful war of independence in the American colonies, and fuelling the French Revolution, an alternative conception made an appearance and quickly gained currency, even dominance, in England. This is the conception that came to be identified as classical liberal in character and that we today would naturally describe as neo-liberal or libertarian.

In 1776, Richard Lind, a pamphleteer writing on behalf of the British prime minister, Lord North, first introduced the new idea of freedom.

15 T.W. Moody, R.B. McDowell & C.J. Woods (eds), *The writings of Theobald Wolfe Tone, 1763–98* (Oxford, 1998), i, p. 115.   16 Quoted in S. Cronin & R. Roche, *Freedom the Wolfe Tone way* (Tralee, 1973), p. 78.   17 T.W. Moody, R.B. McDowell & C.J. Woods (eds), *The writings of Theobald Wolfe Tone, 1763–98*, (Oxford, 2001), ii, p. 30.

Freedom is 'nothing more or less than the absence of coercion', he said, ascribing this idea, wholly inimical to republican ideas, to 'a very worthy and ingenious friend'. But that means, he then pointed out, that since 'all laws are coercive', the laws themselves take away from people's liberty, even if they do so in the hope of reducing the overall level of coercion. And if that is the case, he asked, what is the complaint of the Americans? They are ruled by law, to be sure, but so are those in Britain and so indeed are those in any society whatsoever.[18]

The earlier view had depicted freedom as the product of a protective, popularly controlled law, whether a law controlled under the mixed constitution, or perhaps in the Rousseauvian fashion. By contrast, this view makes law into the antonym of freedom: a form of coercion, whether of body or will, that reduces the choices available to subjects. This is indeed a new view, as the worthy friend had claimed in a letter to Lind. The friend was Jeremy Bentham and in that letter he reported 'a kind of discovery I had made, that the idea of liberty ... was merely a negative one', and should be defined as 'the absence of restraint'.[19] Bentham's view of freedom may have appeared briefly in Hobbes, but Bentham gave it a sharper definition and a greater importance, making it into 'the cornerstone of my system', as he put it in his letter.

This novel view of freedom was useful for Lind and others in rejecting Richard Price's republican argument against colonialism, even the supposedly gentle colonialism of Westminster in relation to the American colonists. But it probably survived because it also served other purposes in the thinking of Bentham and his utilitarian associates, and in the thinking of a new movement that came to be known as classical liberalism.

Bentham himself was a reformer, committed to a relatively inclusive view of the citizenry, and the new view of freedom was useful in allowing him to argue that the law should cater for the equal freedom of all, without seeming to call for a complete overturning of the status quo. To have called for the equal non-domination of all, women and workers included, would have been utterly radical, requiring the transformation of existing family and master-servant law. But to call for freedom in the sense of an equal escape from interference was not at all so revolutionary. It was possible that a wife or worker could be as free in this sense as the master, notwithstanding their subjection to his will, provided that the master stayed his hand and did not actually impose interference.

18 J. Lind, *Three letters to Dr Price* (London, 1776), pp 24, 17.   19 D.C. Long, *Bentham on liberty* (Toronto, 1977), p. 54.

One prominent utilitarian of the time was William Paley, who exercised a great influence over moral and religious thinking in nineteenth-century Britain. He adopted the new view of freedom in a book published in 1785 that became a required part of the Cambridge syllabus and remained so down to 1925. In making the case for what he cast as a novel view – it jars, he admitted, with 'the usage of common discourse' – he acknowledged that nothing more than freedom in this new, downsized sense could be established for all. Thus, he contrasted it with those accounts of freedom, such as the republican:

> which, by making that essential to civil freedom which is unattainable in experience, inflame expectations that can never be gratified, and disturb the public content with complaints, which no wisdom or benevolence of government can remove.[20]

The new conception of freedom as non-interference or non-coercion may have appealed to the likes of Bentham and Paley for making it possible to be relatively egalitarian without being utterly radical. But it appealed to classical liberals for the fact that it provided a way of justifying the new legal and political order that industrialization was calling into existence. In this new order, great numbers of people moved off the land and, with growing industrialization, scrambled for subsistence jobs in the mines, mills and factories, in various cottage industries, and in the construction of the canals and railways. The conditions of most workers were appalling, even by standards current at the time, and a question that naturally arose was whether the people who endured such conditions could count as free.

The new way of thinking suggested that they could. They may have been subjected to their new masters in the manner of 'wage slaves', as many adherents of the older republican way of thinking insisted.[21] And they may have been forced by fear of death or destitution to accept the conditions of industrial labour. But they were not strictly coerced – they were not press-ganged or threatened – into submission. They made an un-coerced decision to work on the terms their employers offered, even if they had little option but to accept those terms: even if they made the decision, as we would say, under duress. They enjoyed what was celebrated by classical liberals as freedom of contract: a freedom from the active coercion of others, if not from the pressure of their awful situation and urgent needs in deciding to take work under what were often appalling conditions.

---

20 W. Paley, *The works of William Paley*, iv: *The principles of moral and political philosophy* (London, 1825), pp 357, 359.   21 M. Sandel, *Democracy's discontent: America in search of a public philosophy* (Cambridge, MA, 1996), pp 172–4.

Free choices rather than free persons

Although it assumed a conception of the basic liberties or choices that should be protected for all, the republican notion of freedom had focused on the freedom of each person in that domain of choice, and on the requirements for reducing both private and public domination. The newer notion shifted the focus to choices of any kind, suggesting that the free society is one where free choice is maximized: where, in effect, all relations between people are organized, so far as possible, on the basis of negotiation, contract and consent. No matter that such a society is likely to display great inequality, to impose conditions on many where their choices are driven by fear and need, and to give some the position of masters in relation to others. It still answers broadly to classical liberal requirements. It satisfies the mantra, for example, that Robert Nozick formulated in defending a version of the approach: 'From each as they choose, to each as they are chosen.'[22]

With the shift to a focus on the free choice rather than the free person, the new theory of freedom moved concern away from domination, whether private or public in character. It did not matter in this view that you lived under the private domination of a master, provided the master dealt with you contractually and did not impose any actual coercion. And it did not matter in this view that you lived under the public domination of government. The coercion of government is acceptable, however un-controlled, to the extent that it restricts private coercion, facilitates contract and choice, and is kept to the minimal level required for those purposes. Thus, William Paley argued that if it operated in this pattern 'an absolute form of government' would be 'no less free than the purest democracy'.[23]

The shift of focus from person to choice had enormous ramifications for how to conceive of the relation between government or law on the one hand and the freedom of individuals on the other. In the older conception, it was government and law that made freedom possible and accessible for citizens. In the newer it was the contractual free-for-all of the market that made freedom possible. To the extent that government and law went beyond the maintenance of market conditions, then, they took away from people's freedom rather than enhancing it. In this new vision, as Ronald Reagan put it two hundred years later, government is the problem, not the solution.

22 R. Nozick, *Anarchy, state, and utopia* (Oxford, 1974), p. 160. 23 W. Paley, *The principles of moral and political philosophy*, p. 166.

NEO-REPUBLICANISM AND NEO-LIBERALISM

Justice, social and democratic

What would these two ideals of liberty support as principles for the conduct of government in a contemporary society? I assume that each approach would be inclusive in recognizing as full citizens all the adult, able-minded, more or less permanent residents of the society. I pass over the question of how far it should be ready to accept would-be immigrants and refugees into the ranks of the citizenry or more generally how it ought to perform on the global stage.[24] And equally I say nothing on how it would argue for the treatment of children or of those who are not able-minded.

There are two aspects under which any philosophy of government will dictate principles for the organization of society and they can be cast roughly as social justice, on the one side, and democratic justice on the other. A society will be socially just to the extent that it organizes relations between individuals and the corporate bodies that individuals constitute in a way that treats all citizens as equals. And a society will be democratically just to the extent that it organizes relations between citizens and the government that rules over them in a way that treats them as equals. Social justice requires that people should be treated equally and well by the law. Democratic justice requires that the shape of the law should be determined by the people themselves, not by an alien or wholly independent will, however benign that will may be; it should not be determined, for example, by a colonial government.

Every philosophy of government gives its own account of what it is for citizens to enjoy treatment as equals and each applies that account to the horizontal relations of people to one another – the subject of social justice – and to their vertical relations to their government: the subject of democratic justice.

Neo-republican principles of justice

The principles of a neo-republican philosophy of government are readily formulated, in light of our brief history of the ideal it sponsored.

> 1. *Social justice*: The law should identify a common set of basic liberties and enable each to exercise those liberties without private domination by others.

24 See Pettit, *Just freedom* for a more comprehensive overview of the dictates of neo-republican principles in both domestic and international contexts.

2. *Democratic justice*: This law should be framed and implemented by government under a form of popular control that guards against public domination.

What are these principles going to support in practice? The principle of social justice is obviously going to require institutions, supported under law, that provide each citizen with a range of security: basic security against aggression, of course, but also educational security, social security, medical security, judicial security, workplace security and the shared securities associated with provisions for food reliability, public health, environmental sustainability, and indeed the defence of the country.

How far should the state secure people in these and other areas? An established republican theme can be of help here. This is the age-old association between being a free, un-dominated person and being able to look others in the eye without reason for fear or deference. If the law can deliver a world that passes or comes close to passing this eyeball test of social justice, then it ought to appeal to the most demanding among us. That world may allow for material inequalities and it may have to restrict some individual securities for the sake of the system overall – for example, it may have to temper workplace security if that is necessary to increase employment – but it will still deliver a palpable and palpably attractive ideal.

What does the neo-republican principle of democratic justice require? There is more to be said in this context than is possible here but it should suffice to point out some of the more obvious preconditions: an electoral system in which each has an equal part; a parliamentary system in which the executive is held properly to account; a strict separation of judicial from other power; a system in which decisions where elected officials have a special interest are put at arm's length from parliament; a campaign system in which politicians do not have to put themselves in the debt of the wealthy; a balanced media that operates under a guarantee of freedom of information; a lobby system in which the grounds and modes of pressure exerted upon government are forced into the public eye; a system of contestation, formal and otherwise, in which all may play an uninhibited part; and a network of public-interest, watchdog bodies that can keep government on its toes.

On this account of democratic justice, government involves a variety of modular measures, as we may call them. First, the separation of powers, as in the distinction between at least the legislative-executive power and the judicial. Second, the sharing of powers as in the distinction between two or more centres of legislation or the hierarchy of appeal among different levels of judicial bodies. Third, the outsourcing of executive power to ensure against short-term, electorally motivated interests of legislators in drawing electoral boundaries, in reducing the interest rates at which money is available to their constituents, or in massaging public information and statistics in the interests of their party. Fourth, the possibility of removing government in the collective election of legislative and perhaps other officials. And fifth, the possibility of people as individuals or in organized groups contesting government directly or indirectly in parliament, in courts, in ombudsmen's offices, in the media or on the streets.

The modular measures of democratic justice canvassed here reflect the strong emphasis in the Roman republican tradition on the importance of having a mixed constitution, as it was called, in which power is separated, shared and in general dispersed across many different authorities. The only prominent figure in the tradition who did not subscribe to this idea, as we saw, was Rousseau. Influenced by the anti-republican critique of the mixed constitution by absolutists like Jean Bodin and Thomas Hobbes, he thought that the only prospect for democratic justice, as we would think of it, is to invest absolute power in an assembly of all the citizens. He argued in *The social contract* of 1762 that the checks and balances hailed in the older tradition would be unnecessary, so long as the members of the assembly restricted themselves to framing general laws, were properly informed on relevant issues and deliberated as citizens, asking in each case after whether 'it is advantageous to the state', not to themselves, 'that this or that opinion pass' (4.1.6).[25]

Our experience today of autocratic democracies suggests strongly that it would be a mistake to follow the Rousseauvian cue: it would be to rely incautiously on the virtue of politicians rather than on the discipline of appropriate institutions. Better economize on virtue, relying on it only when that is inescapable.[26] Better stick with the mixed constitution, albeit not necessarily in the extreme version of the US constitution.

Neo-liberal principles of justice

And now consider the corresponding principles that a neo-liberal philosophy would support.

> 1. *Social justice*: The law should establish a market that facilitates contract and choice, imposing the minimal system of coercive protection that this requires.

25 Gourevitch (ed.), *Rousseau: the social contract.*   **26** See G. Brennan & A. Hamlin, 'Economizing on virtue', *Constitutional Political Economy*, 6 (1995), 35–6; and G. Brennan & P. Pettit, *The economy of esteem: an essay on civil and political society* (Oxford, 2004).

2. *Democratic justice*: This law should be controlled in such a way – presumptively, but not necessarily, in such a democratic way – that people's contractual freedom is maximized.

These principles point in a very different direction from their neo-republican counterparts. The principle of social justice would support a minimal state apparatus for ensuring law and order and within that framework it would argue for letting the market go where it will, even should this lead to extreme inequality, great imbalances of power, and multiple sites of domination. What remedies should apply in cases where the market does not lift the destitute or dependent out of their penury? The answer often proposed is: the remedies to be provided by the private philanthropy of the rich. Even if it fosters domination, as the haves lord it over the have-nots, philanthropy will ensure the satisfaction of Nozick's principle: from each as they choose, to each as they are chosen.

Where does the neo-liberal principle of democratic justice point? As Paley already noticed, and as those advocating China's neo-liberal reforms are well aware, it does not strictly require democracy. All that it requires is that system, whatever it is, that most reliably delivers the market-centred vision of social justice. Alexander Pope may best articulate the bottom line: 'For forms of government let fools contend. Whatever is *best administered is best.*' To be fair, many neo-liberals strongly believe that democracy is likely to be essential for the well-ordered market society that they cherish. But the linkage that they make to democracy is still much weaker than in the alternative picture and, apart from supporting the independence of the judiciary, it offers little in the way of specifications for how democracy itself should be ordered.

CONCLUSION

This brief account of the history of republican and liberal ideas, and of the rival ways of thinking represented by neo-republican and neo-liberal approaches, should indicate the greater appeal of the former.

Neo-republicanism offers a distinctive and attractive view of democratic justice, unlike the neo-liberal approach, or indeed liberal approaches in general. Thus, Isaiah Berlin, who espoused the liberal notion of freedom as non-interference, could write that on this approach the 'connection between democracy and individual liberty is a good deal more tenuous than it has seemed to many advocates of both.'[27] It should be no surprise that a

27 I. Berlin, *Four essays on liberty* (Oxford, 1969), pp 130–1.

country like China should be able to espouse the neo-liberal conception of
freedom without any embarrassment, or at least without any acknowledged
embarrassment, about rejecting standard democratic measures.

How do the two philosophies compare on the issue of social justice, where
more attention is normally given to the divide between them? The republican
approach is far more egalitarian, although not requiring strict equality in the
distribution of resources or in anything so material. The equality it prizes is
social in character, since the index of when it obtains is that people are able
to pass the eyeball test: that they are able to look one another in the eye
without reason for fear or deference.[28]

This sort of equality is essential for people to enjoy dignity and respect,
yet it does not jeopardize the prospects for a free market, as neo-liberal critics
are likely to allege. Neo-liberalism would look for a society where people's
competition with one another is a free-for-all in which the winners take most
of the spoils. Neo-republicanism would seek a society in which economic and
related forms of competition are certainly allowed, but only within limits that
ensure against the dependency and humiliation of weaker members.

In concluding this discussion, I should emphasize that the neo-
republicanism I support, while deeply hostile to neo-liberal or libertarian
thought, actually supports many of the themes defended by liberals in the
broader usage of that term: liberals, for example, in the American sense of
the name. This is not surprising, for the core neo-republican idea that
freedom depends on the law echoes a theme in many of the heroes of such
liberals: heroes that might be better cast indeed as republicans. Thus, John
Locke could write that 'where there is no law there is no freedom' and
Immanuel Kant that it is only 'a lawful constitution' that 'secures everyone
his freedom by laws'.[29] That our freedom as citizens depends on the law that
we collectively create, with a view to our protection as individuals, may be
anathema to contemporary neo-liberals. But it is the common property of
republicans and of liberals in the more encompassing, humane version of
liberalism.

---

28 The social character of republican freedom appears in the fact that people are required
to enjoy the same status as one another in being adequately protected – protected to the
degree required by the eyeball test – against private and public domination. On social
egalitarianism see E. Anderson, 'What is the point of equality?', *Ethics*, 109 (1999), 287–
337 and S. Scheffler, 'Choice, circumstance and the value of equality', *Politics, Philosophy
and Economics*, 4 (2005), 5–28.   29 J. Locke, *Two treatises of government* (Cambridge,
1960), second treatise, section 57; and I. Kant, *Practical philosophy*, trans. M.J. Gregor
(Cambridge, 1996), p. 297.

The promise of 1916: radicalism, radicalization and resettlement, 1916–2016

ROY FOSTER

Philip Pettit and also Iseult Honohan, who responded to Pettit's paper, have drawn our attention to the importance of definitions and names, and naming the Irish revolution has been a complicated matter. Early on, those displaced by the events of 1912–22, or hostile to them used the word 'revolution' to describe what had happened: the *locus classicus* being the book by the Trinity historian W. Alison Phillips, *The revolution in Ireland* (1923). Phillips, who saw himself as representing the losers, was in no doubt that there had been a revolution. The winners were less inclined towards the word, especially in the aftermath of the Russian Revolution. A deliberate preference for the phrase 'war of independence' helped to align the Irish process towards a noble American precedent; it also emphasized that what mattered was indeed liberation from British rule rather than any promise of a new form of social organization, or the elevation of a new class. And indeed, many at the time agreed with the Cork republican activist Liam de Róiste, who said that he had no preference for how Ireland was governed – as a monarchy, a republic or a socialist state – 'so long as it is free from British rule'.[1] This marks a point where nationalism, as Philip Pettit has pointed out, occupies a different space from neo-republicanism.

Nonetheless, there were more ideological visions at work during the period; perhaps one of the less noticed phenomena of the years before and after 1916 is the extent to which the radical ideas of Sinn Féin, as well as those of labour and feminist activists, became muffled or sidelined by the upheavals attendant upon military struggle. We now use the word 'revolution' more easily; a conference in Queen's University Belfast, about fifteen years ago, organized by Joost Augusteijn and the late Peter Hart, was devoted to the question of nomenclature, and concluded that what happened was indeed a revolution if, perhaps, not in the way that we normally know it.[2] This may not get us much further than an attempt to analyze and decode a

---

1 Diary for 20 Mar. 1906, Cork City Archives 271/A/10; quoted in R. Foster, *Vivid faces: the revolutionary generation in Ireland, 1890–1923* (London, 2014), p. 329. 2 The papers read at this conference are published in J. Augusteijn (ed.), *The Irish revolution, 1913–1923* (Basingstoke, 2002).

revolutionary impetus, and come to terms with what happens after it. Was 1916 a revolutionary putsch – or was it a stage in a continuum that stretched from 1912 to 1922? And if so, one of the questions worth asking is whether there was a 'revolution within the revolution', to disinter the 1960s phrase of Regis Debray. In other words, we might ask if the opening of the Anglo–Irish war in 1919 advanced to the fore a different kind of revolutionary to the ideologues who had created what Yeats called a 'stir of thought' in the years before 1916.[3] Some of those ideologues certainly thought so, and would later feel sidelined. It might even be argued that this process began as soon as 1916 changed things utterly. The seismic event of the Rising can be seen as the end of something, as well as the beginning.

Another associated concept concerns viewing what was happening in Ireland as part of a wider dislocation. Some arresting recent work on the period has seen the Irish revolution and civil war as decisively shaped by the Great War, indeed as a theatre of that war; I'm thinking here particularly of the work of the late and much-missed Keith Jeffery.[4] Similarly, Robert Gerwarth's recent book *The vanquished*, and other work by John Horne and himself, posits that the First World War did not end in 1918, but that the break-up of empires that it set in motion created continuing theatres of war and revolution all over Central and Eastern Europe, with paramilitary initiatives, the shifting and changing of borders, and inter-communal conflict.[5] Both Gerwarth and Horne have pointed out that from this perspective, what was happening in Ireland from 1919 to 1923 is very much in line with what was happening elsewhere. I'm reminded that, long before, John Stuart Mill remarked that Ireland's experience was in the mainstream of European history, where England's was in an eccentric tributary.[6]

One thing that has been made clear by recent scholarship, especially by labour historians such as Pádraig Yeates and Emmet O'Connor, is that various forms of radicalism were on offer in the revolutionary period. Social and feminist historians such as Senia Pašeta and Catriona Crowe have broadened the picture to suggest that early twentieth-century Ireland saw a period of destabilization in all sorts of areas – labour relations, religion,

---

3 In his lecture accepting the Nobel Prize in 1923. 'The modern literature of Ireland, and indeed all that stir of thought which prepared for the Anglo-Irish war, began when Parnell fell from power in 1891. A disillusioned and embittered Ireland turned from parliamentary politics; an event was conceived; and the race began, as I think, to be troubled by that event's long gestation.' W.B. Yeats, *Autobiographies* (London, 1955), p. 559.   4 K. Jeffery, *1916: a global history* (London, 2015).   5 R. Gerwarth, *The vanquished: why the First World War failed to end, 1917–1923* (London, 2016); R. Gerwarth & John Horne (eds), *War in peace: paramilitary violence after the Great War* (Oxford, 2012).   6 J.S. Mill, *England and Ireland* (London, 1868), *passim*, but especially

gender relations, the family – besides nationalist politics, though it's the latter that (until recently) monopolized attention.[7] Sinn Féin was very much a youth movement, and the idea of generational shift, and a revolt against parental and establishment values, was fused (in the case of some influential revolutionaries) with a rebellion against the British empire.

We have to avoid wishful thinking, and retrospective projection of what we would have liked to be true. But the sources that have been opened up by the digitization of newspapers, Bureau of Military History (BMH) witness statements, military service pension records and so on, invoked at this symposium by both NUIG President James Browne and Seán Ó Foghlú, the secretary general to the Department of Education and Skills, present a suggestive picture. Through these sources we may disinter forgotten agendas, and recapture a distinctly radical voice that is also secularist, feminist and social-democratic if not socialist – in line, again, with opinion among the younger generation elsewhere in Europe during the 1900s. I've made this case at length elsewhere, though my old friend, the distinguished Galway historian Gearóid Ó Tuathaigh has mischievously remarked to me that when examining a picture of republican activists in Athenry in 1916, he found it hard to discern *poètes maudits* and lesbian socialists; I told him not to be so sure.[8]

Student societies, and the part played by the new National University, constitute another area of research that has been opened up in recent years. It seems that from 1916, the rhetoric of radical nationalism took over and replaced those other rhetorics: a process amplified by the 'Catholicization' of the revolution. The *Catholic Bulletin*, under J.J. O'Kelly's editorship, adopted the signatories of the Proclamation as saints, placing them firmly into the tradition of early Irish Christianity, where lives of self-denial and fortitude were celebrated, along with the themes of renunciation and the redemption of mankind. This followed the model laid down in Pearse's eloquent speeches and writings, and Pearse's mother indeed forecast that the day would come when her sons' bones would be 'lifted as they were the bones of saints'. This had not been the objective of all of the revolutionaries, who were in several cases a good deal more hard-headed and secular-minded than the company of saints; some of them, like Bulmer Hobson, would later remember – sadly – what fun they had had in their revolutionary youth.[9]

pp 8–9, 15–16.   **7** See, among much else, P. Yeates, *Lockout: Dublin, 1913* (Dublin, 2001); *A city in wartime: Dublin 1914–1918* (Dublin, 2011); *A city in turmoil: Dublin, 1919–1921* (Dublin, 2012); E. O'Connor, *A labour history of Ireland, 1824–2000* (Dublin, 2011); S. Pašeta, *Irish nationalist women, 1900–1918* (Cambridge, 2013); C. Crowe, *Dublin, 1911* (Dublin, 2011).   **8** See my *Vivid faces, passim.*   **9** 'I wonder how many people

'Fun', not to mention secularism, was understandably at a discount in the transfigured state of existence after the executions of 1916. But the Irish revolution took place against a background of upheaval in hearts and minds that characterized Europe before 1914, one of those generational shifts of tempo that happened in France in the 1780s, or the USA in the 1960s, whereby a generation sees itself in sharp contradistinction to the 'acceptance world' of their parents, and attempts to project change into the world at large, from the change that they have asserted within their personality. I have written about this in a recent book, and will leave it there. But it does seem to me that there was a distinct shift in the *kind* of revolution that had been in prospect before 1916, and the actuality of armed struggle after the event. The conscription crisis in 1918 completed the process, allowing clerics to share platforms with Sinn Féin (and the increasingly outflanked Irish Parliamentary Party). This laid the ground for Sinn Féin's success in 1918. It also helped condition the kind of Ireland that would emerge after independence.

As the Anglo-Irish war got under way, faith-and-fatherland nationalist tropes predominated over socialist or feminist initiatives, a process strongly reinforced by the ascendancy of Cumann na nGaedheal and the marginalization of many pre-revolutionary radicals, whose disillusionment can be clearly tracked. Prominent examples include Bulmer Hobson, Patrick McCartan, P.S. O'Hegarty, Rosamund Jacob, Hanna Sheehy-Skeffington and Seán Ó Faoláin. 'Freedom' was bitterly argued and contested. Philip Pettit's contribution to this symposium raised the question of the liberal definition of freedom. This is exactly what John Redmond, the home rule leader, tried to present in a speech in 1915, appealing to his audience to be 'sensible and truthful' and admit that the incremental reforms of the previous decades had made the Irish a free people.[10] At that very time, however, to a young republican such as Geraldine Plunkett, the Irish people were living in conditions of 'actual slavery' – despite her own position of wealth and privilege.[11] The invocation of freedom meant very different things to the two generations.

There were other forms of liberation at issue too. Senia Pašeta's recent book has shown how central the suffrage issue was in drawing many women into political activism in the early 1900s (and in alienating them from the Irish Parliamentary Party). We should also remember that the 1898 reform

nowadays get so much fun as we did?': to Denis McCullough, 1 Sept. 1965, quoted in M. Hay, *Bulmer Hobson and the nationalist movement in twentieth-century Ireland* (Manchester, 2009), p. 246. 10 Quoted in my *Vivid faces*, p. 2. 11 Ibid., pp 23–4.

of local government in Ireland not only democratized and nationalized local government, but enfranchised about 100,000 women and made them eligible to stand in local elections – another process of politicization (and an unintended consequence of British government in Ireland). For such people, the limited opportunities for women in the Ireland of the 1920s and 1930s were very far from the promise of 1916.

Significantly, the subject of post-revolutionary disillusionment among dissident Irish intellectuals has emerged as part of the cultural history of the era, notably in a recent book by Frances Flanagan.[12] So has the way that the organization of Dáil Éireann managed the complex processes of local government in matters of clientelism and finance, charted some time ago by Arthur Mitchell and Tom Garvin, and also in Brian Hughes' absorbing new book about the relationship between the IRA and the civilian community during the revolution.[13] This too laid important groundwork for the way the new state evolved – as did the remarkable speed with which police and army authorities were reconstituted, against a background of violence and antagonism. A lively debate has sprung up about the meaning of 'democracy' as established in the Irish Free State, and the competing notions of politics at the time.[14] Another important historiographical development has seen a concentration on what violence, coercion and intimidation meant at local levels.[15]

The restabilization of the 1920s was paralleled in some other European countries that had experienced violent paramilitary activity; social conservatism, a turn towards censorship, and a deep-rooted fear of communism, were not peculiar to Ireland. But one very important factor influencing the way things developed was that there had already been a quiet revolution in landholding, precipitated by the Land War of 1879–81 and sustained by the government policy of enabling tenants to purchase their holdings. As one revolutionary (John Marcus O'Sullivan) noted, this had had the effect of curtailing the impulses towards social radicalism among those

12 F. Flanagan, *Remembering the revolution: dissent, culture and nationalism in the Irish Free State* (Oxford, 2015).   13 A. Mitchell, *Revolutionary government in Ireland: Dáil Éireann, 1919–1922* (Dublin, 1995); T. Garvin, *1922: the birth of Irish democracy* (Dublin, 1996); B. Hughes, *Defying the IRA? Intimidation, coercion and communities during the Irish revolution* (Liverpool, 2016).   14 See, e.g., J. Praeger, *Building democracy in Ireland: political order and cultural integration in a newly independent nation* (Cambridge, 1986); B. Kissane, *The politics of the Irish civil war* (Oxford, 2003); Garvin, op. cit.   15 Hughes, op. cit.; G. Clark, *Everyday violence in the Irish civil war* (Cambridge, 2014); P. Hart, *The IRA and its enemies: violence and community in Cork, 1916–1923* (Oxford, 1998); and *The IRA at war, 1916–1923* (Oxford, 2003); T. Wilson, *Frontiers of violence: conflict and identity in Ulster and Upper Silesia, 1918–1922* (Oxford, 2010).

directing the political revolution against British rule. 'It is well for us that the two revolutions, through which we have passed in the last half-century, were separate in time; that, in fact, the agrarian revolution was largely at an end before the struggle for national independence became fully acute. Had the two coincided, the outlook would indeed be menacing.'[16]

The conservative nature of Irish society was underwritten by the power of the Catholic church in social as well as political terms, a syndrome reinforced (or even enabled) by the partition of Ireland, which made the Free State, and later the Republic, an almost entirely Catholic unit, with a very small minority of Protestants. These rapidly accepted the status of the new political entity and, initially at least, played a part in its commercial, economic and professional life disproportionate to their numbers. The Irish Free State provided a much 'warmer house', to borrow David Trimble's phrase, for its tiny Protestant minority than Northern Ireland did for its large Catholic minority – though there was nonetheless a disproportionate exodus of Protestants from the south in the immediate aftermath of independence.[17] How different a thirty-two-county Ireland with a large (perhaps 25 per cent) minority Protestant population would have been is an intriguing counterfactual; Tom Garvin has suggested that, if partition had not happened, we would have to look to the Balkans in the 1990s for an Irish parallel, but others might be less pessimistic.[18] What also made Ireland's path to a certain extent *sui generis* was partly the power of the Catholic church and the almost-monolithic religious composition of the populace, as well as the rapid development of a widely accepted unarmed police force and a small and carefully regulated army. But there was also the implicit continuity of themes and forms of government inherited from the years of British rule. Despite ambitions for a different dispensation, a two-party democratic and bicameral parliamentary system evolved, with a powerful and independent civil service. Despite a radically redrawn constitution in 1937, many legal forms and practices also bore strong family resemblances to Britain. Here is another area where the ideas of Sinn Féin fade into the background – even economic protectionism, given the position of Ireland within the Commonwealth, took a back seat during the 1920s, until it was rediscovered *faute de mieux* by de Valera during the economic war of the 1930s.

16 Quoted in J. Regan, *The Irish counter-revolution, 1921–1936* (Dublin, 1999), p. 378.
17 This development has been recently examined by D. Fitzpatrick in *Descendancy: Irish Protestant histories since 1765* (Cambridge, 2014) and by A. Bielenberg, 'Exodus: the emigration of southern Irish Protestants during the Irish war of independence and the civil war', *Past and Present*, 218:1 (Feb. 2013), 199–233.   18 Garvin, op. cit., p. 24.

Speaking recently at the Irish centre in Camden Town, London, I was asked why the Irish revolution produced such a stable state, unlike other post-First World War revolutions in Central Europe and elsewhere. My answer was: for the same reason that the revolution succeeded in the first place, that is, that the revolutionaries had the good fortune to be rebelling against a liberal democratic state, unlike the dissolving empires elsewhere in Europe. One outcome was Britain's responsiveness to domestic public opinion, which pushed Lloyd George to terms. Another outcome was that very stability which my questioner mentioned – which arose – as just outlined – from the fact that the new state mimicked so many of the legal, political and cultural forms of the British government ethos. This was not the romantic utopia preached by the 1916 revolutionaries, but it was effective nonetheless. And, moreover, it moved very swiftly to accommodating and friendly relations with the ex-oppressor. This was what enabled the cynical Arthur Balfour (in the past a chief secretary of Ireland as well as a Tory prime minister) to observe, in the late 1920s, 'the Ireland of today is the Ireland we made'.[19]

It also seems to me that the emphasis on historical victimhood and oppression, so marked in the rhetoric of the revolution, obscures the fact that in Edwardian Ireland the obvious forms of oppression by 'England' were in the past. While condescension and various forms of exclusion continued, the changes in land ownership, taxation reform, local-government reform, old-age pensions, and the clientelist hegemony of the Irish Parliamentary Party were creating in Ireland a materialist, Anglophone world against which the idealism of the revolutionary generation rebelled. Here again we encounter the two different notions of 'freedom', liberal and republican, and the implicit conflict between them.

These were not very well received ideas when I shared them with the Camden Irish centre, and another audience member truculently remarked that all Ireland's post-revolutionary problems arose from the fact that the country hadn't adopted 'a truly Gaelic form of government'. I didn't ask whether this meant reversion to the Brehon laws and the institution of high-kings. But the concept raises what Jeffrey Prager would call the 'Gaelic-Romantic' versus 'Irish-Enlightenment' tropes that were argued out in the aftermath of revolution. This dichotomy can be queried, but the caution and subtlety with which the constitutions of the Free State, and then of 'Éire' were drawn up, deserves recognition: it was noted some time ago particularly that the 1922 constitution cleverly incorporated elements of a nascent

19 See B.E.C. Dugdale, *Arthur James Balfour* (London, 1936), ii, p. 392.

republican status into a framework formally designed to exist within the Commonwealth.[20] The conservatism of the post-revolutionary state may be too easily decried; the power of the church in matters of state, and the implicit continuities from the era of British rule, made for social stability during an era of European upheaval in the 1930s and 1940s. However, neither factor could be openly acknowledged, and conservative Irish administrations operated within strict and coded parameters (with a partial exception when the Clann na Poblachta party in government looked like it would break the mould in the late 1940s). The prevalence of large-scale emigration, especially of the young, helped to sustain this stasis. So did the low-key state of industrial unionization (and of industry altogether).

The breaking up of the post-revolutionary dispensation has been much debated, along with the meaning of 'modernization', Irish-style, which Joe Lee and others have stimulatingly projected back into the aftermath of the Famine in the mid- to late nineteenth century. More predictably, the influence and chronology of the shift to economic liberalization from the late 1950s used to be taken as a *sine qua non*, along with the belated emergence of Seán Lemass as a modern-minded taoiseach, following the lengthy years of de Valera's ascendancy. Later perspectives, notably a recent book by Mary Daly, take a more sociological and less high-political view, seeing Ireland's trajectory as part of a 'global moment' in the 1960s that brought both liberalization and instability – as well as a more limited degree of economic and social transformation than often assumed.[21] Here we might also note recent treatments of the Northern Ireland crisis, by Prince, Warner and others, which stress the early 1960s as a time of cautious reconciliation and liberalization, derailed by the events of 1968–9 and after.[22] In the Republic, the 1960s certainly ushered in a period of interrogation and reassessment, featuring the women's movement and a challenging of religious and patriarchal authority. This is notable, following as it did the uncomplicatedly triumphalist fiftieth-anniversary celebrations of 1916 in 1966.

How many of the 'promises' of the 1916 revolutionary generation had been put on ice for the ensuing half-century, and to what extent can the students' and women's movements of the 1960s and 1970s be seen as a revival

---

20 L. Kohn, *The constitution of the Irish Free State* (London, 1932) is still useful, but see especially C. Townshend, 'The meaning of Irish freedom: constitutionalism in the Free State', *Transactions of the Royal Historical Society*, 6th ser., 7 (1998), 45–70.   21 M.E. Daly, *Sixties Ireland: reshaping the economy, state and society, 1957–1973* (Cambridge, 2016).   22 S. Prince & G. Warner, *Belfast and Derry in revolt: a new history of the start of the Troubles* (Dublin, 2012); S. Prince, *Northern Ireland's '68: civil rights, global revolt and the origins of the Troubles* (Dublin, 2007). Many of Seamus Heaney's recollections in

or even rediscovery of some of the *élan vital* of the revolutionary generation? That is necessarily an open question, but reading the language, concerns and responses of the Edwardian generation of Irish radicals, as recorded in their letters, diaries and journalism, the tone is sometimes oddly predictive of the 1960s generation. That generation, at least in France and the USA, has now become the object of large-scale academic collaborative research projects – often asking the question that Augusta Gregory posed about the 1916 rebels in a thoughtful unpublished essay of 1916, 'What was their utopia?' (That essay was, by the way, an important influence – I believe – on the gestation of Yeats' canonical poem about the Rising, 'Easter 1916'.)

It is striking that in the huge corpus of testaments gathered by the Bureau of Military History from 1947 to 1957, the old revolutionaries consistently remembered the impetus for their actions as coming from memories of historical oppression, rather than economic immiseration or liberationist ideologies derived from socialism or feminism – though these motivations are amply recorded in contemporary documentation from the revolutionary period. It is true that several people who were thus motivated refused to provide witness statements for the bureau, but I think we are also seeing here the complex way that historical memory operates.[23]

Imagined utopias are part of any revolutionary impetus, for better or worse. And – for better or worse – they rarely survive the onset of an economic boom, as would overtake Ireland in the 1990s. The anti-materialist ethos preached by de Valera, Liam Mellows and others during the revolution and the austere approach to public spending and balancing the books embraced by the Cumann na nGaedheal governments of the 1920s had instituted an ethos that helped – among other things – accustom independent Ireland to the idea that ostentatious prosperity was incompatible with true autonomy and – in de Valera's words – a Christian and Gaelic way of life. The idea mooted by some Sinn Féin ideologues in the early twentieth century – that prosperity *was* compatible with independent Irishness, given a new approach to corporate economics and commercial policy, was allowed to recede into history. This may have been for the best, in some ways at least, but it did leave the awkward question of Ireland's dependence upon the British market unanswered.

A partial answer was provided by the expansion of Ireland's availability to inward investment, pioneered by the Industrial Development Authority (IDA) from the 1950s, and the continued expansion of multinational

D. O'Driscoll (ed.), *Stepping stones: interviews with Seamus Heaney* (London, 2008) suggest the same.   **23** See *Vivid faces*, ch. 9.

companies in Ireland from the 1990s, with associated taxation incentives. But the essential background to prosperity was Ireland's joining the European Economic Community in 1973, with the attendant inward flow of money for infrastructural investments of various sorts. The roller-coaster of prosperity, the replacement of emigration by immigration, and the less desirable concomitants of Wild West banking practices and an unsustainable boom in building and property, are very recent history.[24] But it is worth relating them to the ideas and ideals of a hundred years ago, since they form the backdrop to any twenty-first-century assessment of how Ireland stands in relation to its history, and to the wider world.

The fact that the background to Ireland's recent boom and bust involved an expansion of psychological as well as economic borders to the wider world is a central issue. One of the 'promises' of independence was an end to the kind of poverty thought inseparable from colonial rule. Yet, as historians such as Cormac Ó Gráda and Tom Garvin have trenchantly shown, Ireland stayed poor after 1922. Indeed, de Valera had to effectively make a virtue of it, presenting it as an inseparable and even desirable part of Irish purity.[25] Prosperity only came when Ireland once again joined a larger unit of government, the European Economic Community, later the European Union. This was mostly seen as an enhancement of independent sovereignty rather than a diminution of it, until rogue bankers and corrupt developers ruined the economy, and economic sovereignty was handed over to Brussels as the price of the bailout.

This recent trauma was implicitly influential in the way that commemoration happened in the 'decade' that officially began in 2012. So was the fact that over the previous decades the Catholic church had lost so much moral, social and political authority, compared to 1966. How much of the 'promise' of 1916 has been belatedly redeemed, and at what cost?

Recent history and current political considerations have always inflected the way we commemorate independence and its promises, both this year and in other years. As Mary Daly and others have incisively shown, the question of commemoration came sharply into focus from the early years of the new Irish State in the 1920s, massaged and manipulated by civil servants, claimed by politicians, furiously reacted to by old revolutionaries or their relicts, who felt sidelined and repudiated.[26] This was the result of a contested history, and

24 Considered in my *Luck and the Irish: a brief history of change, c.1970–2000* (London, 2007); also note the many salient points in the 'Conclusion' to Daly, op. cit.   25 C. Ó Gráda, *A rocky road: the Irish economy since independence* (Manchester, 1997) and *Ireland: a new economic history, 1780–1939* (Oxford, 1994); T. Garvin, *Preventing the future: why was Ireland so poor for so long?* (Dublin, 2004).   26 M. Daly & M. O'Callaghan (eds),

the unstated but continuing conflicts of the civil war, raising the central question of what the revolution had been fought for and who had inherited it – and reflecting those implicit tensions that I have been talking about. Those in power used commemorative activities to stress militarism, conveying the message of independent power. (This despite the fact that the army had become – in the words of one historian – 'a tiny internal security force combined with a squad of mounted ceremonial hussars and a jumping team'.)[27] But there were less obvious demonstrations at work too. The fiftieth anniversary of 1916, celebrated in 1966, was a matter not only of triumphalism but of diplomatic evasion and frantic behind-the-scenes brinkmanship, as to who was 'in' and who was 'out'. The public spectacle of fly-pasts and demonstrations, and the survival of some of the principals of those stirring events fifty years before, notably Éamon de Valera, both added to the mystique and raised awkward questions. This was sharply put in focus when de Valera and others used the commemorations to invoke a wish to complete the revolution by ending partition and 'reuniting' the country. By the time of the seventy-fifth anniversary in 1991, however, given what was actually happening in Northern Ireland, a low-key approach was taken, covering up disagreements behind the scenes – particularly between Taoiseach Haughey, once accused of supplying guns to the Provos, and President Mary Robinson, who had made a particular cause of listening to the unionist case.

Thus partition remained the elephant in the room. It would later be claimed that rhetorical revanchism in the Republic helped galvanize unionist resistance in the North, threatening burgeoning liberalization in that deeply divided province. That is a vexed question, though I have already noted that some recent historiography emphasizes the early 1960s as a time when old moulds were being broken, and relations between the two communities moving towards cautious accommodation. The eruption from 1969 changed everything utterly, and the horrors to follow would entrench the border more firmly than ever before. What they meant for memory and history in the island of Ireland is an enormous subject, and not a central part of this lecture. But this much is relevant. The romantic faith-and-fatherland story of Irish liberation through sacrificial revolution, with its heroic frieze of saints and martyrs, and its assumption that there was one true church of Irish identity, had already been powerfully queried in academic historiography since the late 1930s – it is a subject that has recently received much scholarly attention. Robin Dudley Edwards dared to suggest, exactly sixty years ago, that a necessary part of Irish national maturity must mean being able to ask whether 1916 was an unequivocally good thing:

> As long as our recent history is presented as a one-sided justification of the roles played by our leaders in 1922, so long will it be impossible to make it palatable to the children … Until it is clear to the meanest intelligence that one can be a good Irishman and disagree with Fianna Fáil or Fine Gael or even with the Rising of 1916, Irish unity will continue to be a vain hope.[28]

But questioning the Manichean dualities of the received version of Irish history remained largely within the scholarly community until the North blew apart at the end of the 1960s.

Why a revisionist and often iconoclastic approach to Irish history advanced into prominence from the 1970s clearly had much to do with the use being made of 'history' by combatants in the North – though it also, I think, indicated the influence of wider historiographical influences from abroad. The 'history from below' ideas of left-wing British social historians, the ideas of the *Annales* school in France, the new social and intellectual history prospected by a brilliant generation of American historians – all this did not go unnoticed in Ireland, and propelled Irish historians to see the country's history in a less essentialist way, at least in the Republic. The continued adherence to Manichean dualities of historical worldview (or nation-view) north of the border is, I think, one of the ways in which a cultural divide has not yet been crossed. Another strong influence – as I see it – though it's not much mentioned, was a shift in Irish cultural attitudes (among the young at least) away from the obediently religious cast of mind that had inflected the interpretation of national history, a shift that had much to do with the advent of radical feminism in the early 1970s.[29] Here again we might discern a revival of the preoccupations that had motivated at least some revolutionaries, a half century before. Faith-and-fatherland views had carried a strong charge of manifest destiny and the veneration of founding fathers; the more existentialist mentality of the 1960s preferred to investigate alternative futures, and to see the past as a series of open questions.

There was a certain reaction in the 1990s, sometimes described at the time as a more poised and self-confident period than the dreary era that preceded it and brought forth revisionism. But now that the gloss has worn off the 'poise and self-confidence' of the Celtic Tiger era, the accompanying readiness to airbrush out awkwardnesses in the national history and proclaim

28 'The future of Fianna Fáil', *Leader*, 29 Jan. 1955.   29 See Daly, *Sixties Ireland*, ch. 9.

a fudged unity between past and present, looks less convincing. There is a sense in which Irish historians have advanced gingerly towards a common ground where nuance is explored and sheep and goats are allowed to mingle together. The commemorations in 2016 have allowed and enabled this, and those of us who were sceptical at the outset must now admit it. It seems clear that 'memory' – that awkward concept which in some fashionable quarters seems to have replaced 'history' – has been explored in a way that, as NUIG President Jim Browne pointed out in his opening address at the conference on which this volume is based, has been allowed complicate the national narrative. This was helped greatly, I think, by the release (and digitization) of the vast first-person sources that have been mentioned already, as well as the realization that there were other narratives and other identifications subscribed to in Ireland a hundred years ago, notably in terms of the vast numbers of Irish people who fought and died in the First World War.

We have also perhaps learned something from other commemorative jamborees in Ireland – such as the 150th anniversary of the onset of the Great Famine in 1995, and the bicentenary of the 1798 Rising in 1998. The memory of the Famine allowed for a certain amount of well-meant but sometimes questionable psychotherapeutic statements about trauma, survivor guilt and collective memory; it was often stated that the catastrophe had imposed a 'silence' on communal memory of that awful time, but anyone who grew up in rural Ireland knew that was not true, and several folklore scholars crisply pointed out as much. There were also a good few theatrical or re-enacted events, of varying effectiveness. More relevantly (and lastingly), a number of Famine museums were created, and local-history investigations led to some genuine advances in historical knowledge and the publication of some pioneering scholarship.

A few years later the bicentenary of 1798 told a rather different story. Again, there were several illuminating exhibitions and some suggestive scholarship brought new light to bear on the violent summer of 1798. But the Irish government of the day took a leading and highly politicized role, galvanized by the peace process then unfolding in the North. The fact that Northern Presbyterians had – two hundred years before – been in the vanguard of revolutionary republican activity was too good to ignore, and a determined effort was made to equate the project of the late-eighteenth-century United Irishmen to the efforts of Irish politicians in the present day: two eras of supposed cross-community reconciliation were breathlessly twinned, and late twentieth-century Eurospeak was applied to the French revolutionary connections of the rebels. The political use of historical parallels tends to completely discount questions of context and change.

We've seen this very vividly these last cliffhanging months, with Donald Trump's supporters paralleling his utter lack of experience in any elected office to that of Abraham Lincoln; or the equally farfetched claims of British Brexiteers, who compare the decision to leave Europe to the Henrician repudiation of papal authority in the sixteenth century. In the Ireland of 1998, this kind of time travelling meant dismissing the sectarian realities of the late eighteenth century as retrospective rationalizations imposed by the evil Saxon, and airbrushing out incidents of cross-community violence. Thus the impetus was to resolutely uncomplicate the historical narrative, in the interests of present political realities.[30]

This seems to me what the commemorative organizations attending to 1916 in 2016 managed to avoid. The official approach, expressed by the president and the taoiseach, laudably emphasized aspects that are 'inclusive' and celebratory – while also recognizing the countering traditions in Irish politics a hundred years ago, both home ruler and unionist. I might also mention, once again, the way that a new generation of historians has begun to examine the effect of violence on local communities. It should be remembered that revolutionary consciousness is necessarily about extremism, enmity, repudiation and what Yeats roundly called 'fanaticism' and 'hatred'. Not to mention terror and death. This too often means that rationalization of pre-revolutionary conditions plays a large part in official memory – smoothing out awkward, ambiguous, iconoclastic elements, and prioritizing the pietistic and feel-good side. There are also the imperatives of the tourist industry, the branding of 'heritagescapes', and the macabre phenomenon of what has been called 'thanatourism' (concentrating on scenes of death and slaughter). In their efforts to avoid this, the government committee in charge of the commemorations were originally criticized in some quarters for what seemed to be their caution and equivocation, by those who would prefer straightforward celebration, and the assertion of a direct and unproblematic line of descent from the originary moment of 1916 to the political forms of the present day. (Long ago, in the early 1930s, Yeats – no enemy to the aristocratic principle – remarked that in the future, having an ancestor who had been in the General Post Office in 1916 would be tantamount to an American claiming descent from someone who sailed on the Mayflower, and so it has proved.)

But at the same time, it must be admitted that commemorating 1916 is different from remembering the Famine, or 1798. Those events were, in different ways, disasters, representing tragedy and failure on a national scale.

---

30 I have considered these issues at more length in my *The Irish story: telling tales and making it up in Ireland* (London, 2001).

The 1916 Rising, by contrast, marks a foundational point in the history of the state, and those who planned it are necessarily seen as founders of that state. Though this has been queried in some analyses, it seems to me a given. But there are complicating factors. For one thing, we cannot tell how far the state that emerged after the Anglo-Irish treaty would have been endorsed by the signatories of the proclamation of the republic in 1916, since they were executed. In 'Easter 1916', Yeats wrote, 'We know their dream; enough/To know they dreamed and are dead'. But if we try, from contemporary sources, to get closer to what they actually dreamed – to find out 'What *was* their utopia?' – much of it seems rather far removed from the ethos of the Irish Free State, while some aspects of it have arguably come to fruition in the near-century of independence that has seen the country become what it is today.

Though I have warned against time travelling, part of the commemorative process must mean looking at the ideals of the revolutionaries, as they affect today's Ireland, while making every allowance for differences of context, temporal, cultural and global. We still might consider the ideals of the revolutionaries in terms of equality of opportunity, a genuinely representative government, investment in social issues and cultural capital, and democratic accountability. Regarding the Ireland of 2016, it is generally admitted – or should be – that these priorities were heavily compromised by the continuing effects of the austerity imposed by the philistine excesses and idiocies of the boom. This might deserve more consideration than the sensitivities of those descended from rebels, or the appropriateness of a visit from a member of the House of Windsor. And some of the generous budget set aside for commemorative purposes should certainly be directed towards enhancing – or just rescuing – some of the threatened major cultural institutions of the state. The revolution was created in colleges, theatres and libraries as well as in the General Post Office. Sustaining such places is a more meaningful act of commemoration than ephemeral jamborees and redundant memorial artefacts.

Ireland in 2016 is – inevitably – a very different place from in 1916. We cannot ignore that it looked different again in 2006, just before the crash; and we cannot ignore 'peace walls' in the North and ghost estates in the south; nor the deficit of accountability in certain aspects of Irish public life; nor the fact that the crash-course with Europe recently embarked upon by Britain threatens to impact powerfully upon this country, reminding us that – due to propinquity as well as history – our ancient relationship stubbornly survives, for better or worse. History is being made all around us, and 2016 will be remembered worldwide for far more disruptive events than commemorating a revolution in Ireland.

But it seems to me to be important that we try and recapture in 2016 the wish of the revolutionaries to make a different world – or many different worlds – that did not resemble the restrictive and quasi-theocratic state that emerged in the 1920s. Stable and admirable though it was in many ways, it denied many people the futures that they wanted and expected. The Proclamation stressed equality of status and opportunity as a concomitant of independence from Britain. But the emergence of an Irish 'establishment' was an inevitable part of post-revolutionary history, with the kind of resettlement that created the Ireland we know today.

The new Ireland was, and for most of the twentieth century remained, partitioned, English-speaking, politically conservative, well-educated, and inevitably marked by its proximity to and historical relationship with Britain. By the early twenty-first century, though, models taken from Boston and Berlin seemed more relevant than London, and the European dimension of our recent history dominated the experience of the crash. It was also the context in which Ireland regained some measure of sovereignty after European intervention and sectional economic recovery. The future historian of twenty-first-century Ireland will have to relate this economic roller-coaster to the implications for Ireland of Britain's withdrawal from the European Union, and probably to whatever instability of the world order is now upon us since the recent political tsunami in the USA. That is not my job, I'm thankful to say; and where the ideals and promises of 1916 relate to this scenario is an open question. The revolutionary generation could not have anticipated the uncertainty of Ireland's situation in today's globalized world. But it may explain why so much of this year's concentration on remembering the promise of 1916, and its relevance to Ireland today, has stressed, as the taoiseach memorably did, the country's cultural and artistic achievements. These, less problematically, take us back to the world of the revolutionary generation who wanted to 'make it new' – and partially did.

Culture and globalization: contemporary storytelling and the legacies of 1916

CLAIR WILLS

I have been asked to address the challenges for Irish art and culture in an era of globalization, and the ways in which the current era might differ from, and respond to, previous 'world' moments in the history of Irish literature and culture. I'd like to begin by picking up on a comment made by Roy Foster at the end of his presentation, about the uncertainty of Ireland's position in today's globalized world. He suggested that by comparison with its current political and economic instability, Ireland's cultural and artistic achievements have never been in doubt. I was reminded of that line by W.B. Yeats, thinking back to the possible effect of his play *Cathleen Ni Houlihan*, on the revolutionary generation of 1916: 'Did that play of mine send out certain men the English shot?' And I recalled too Paul Muldoon's rejoinder to Yeats in a rather more recent poem. 'Certain men?' he queried:

'Certainly not'.

If Yeats had saved his pencil-lead
would certain men have stayed in bed?

For history's a twisted root
with art its small, translucent fruit

and never the other way round.

Certainty, fixed positions, unshakeable convictions – these are not qualities we usually associate with literature, art and cultural practice, and for good reason. A simple story of national liberation or national failure has never been part of literature's contribution to the legacy of 1916, and today I want to think about the different ways contemporary cultural practice asks us to keep questioning and opening up national histories. Centenary discussions of the Rising have increasingly located the events of 1916 in international and transnational contexts.[1] But debates about the 1916 Commemorations

---

1 For example, the academic conferences, 'Globalizing the Rising: 1916 in Context', University College Dublin, 5–6 Feb. 2016; 'The 1916 Easter Rising in a global

themselves have continued to focus on a national past: on what the memory of 1916 means for contemporary Ireland, on Irish identity and on the relationship between Ireland and Britain. It is not that this national feeling was orchestrated by the commemorations in any simple sense, but they did offer a means of expressing it. Anyone who was present in Ireland on the Easter bank holiday weekend of 2016 could not fail to have been struck by the palpable feeling of ownership of a national story, and by what felt like a genuinely popular response, particularly in comparison to the more muted, state-organized events of 2006. The difficulty is in knowing how to read that sense of ownership. Is it that 'ordinary people' were always more interested in and proud of the foundation of the state than politicians acknowledged, and now they have been allowed to express it? Or have the current economic pressures on national sovereignty made it appear more valuable?

One of the issues I want to raise here has to do with the balance between national and international or transnational perspectives in contemporary culture.[2] Two fundamental shifts – the economic crash, and the retreat of the Catholic church – have shaped the decade of commemorations in decisive ways. Both these developments have played out across national borders, yet it is their domestic impact that has absorbed cultural commentators, and for obvious reasons. A welcome consequence of this national focus has been to foreground hidden histories of the independent Irish state – it is no longer possible to separate the story of national sovereignty from the story of what was done with that sovereignty, and I am particularly thinking here of the history of clerical and institutional abuse. Indeed one way of thinking about the contemporary moment is that Ireland has shifted from being a secret-keeping to a storytelling nation. Beyond the realm of fiction and drama I am referring to the way that individuals feel more able to tell their own stories, because those stories are now being listened to. Contemporary shock and distress over the revelations concerning mother-and-baby homes, for example, was initially spurred by the discovery of the remains of babies and small children buried in unmarked graves. But the commission of investigation into the homes has also received hundreds of residents' accounts of their experiences, stories that women have, for the most part, been keeping to themselves for decades. While no one could possibly regret these developments, we also need to be alert to the stories that remain buried

perspective: the revolution that succeeded?', Cambridge, 3–5 Mar. 2016.   2 For recent discussions of globalization in relation to contemporary Irish cultural practice see, for example, P. Lonergan, *Theatre and globalization: Irish drama in the Celtic Tiger era* (Basingstoke, 2009); and L. Harte, *Reading the contemporary Irish novel, 1987–2007* (Oxford, 2014).

as others are uncovered. Narratives, after all – as psychoanalysis continually reminds us – are as good at concealing as they are at revealing, though different genres (historical, fictional and autobiographical accounts, for example) carry out the work of concealment in different ways.

Which storylines get forgotten as others are remembered, and how do they get forgotten? In order to approach this question I would like to consider some of the cultural – storytelling – legacies of 1916. In which ways do the idea of the nation, its histories, its boundaries, and its porousness continue to be shaped by debates generated during the revolutionary period? Part of what I wish to explore is the way that certain genres have assumed the weight of 'expressing' Irish national consciousness, as well as thinking about its boundaries and its others. So, my concern is not only with which stories get told, but also with how those stories get told. I want to ask whether some genres may be more or less productive than others in representing national stories. Can the novel, contemporary site-specific performance, mixed media, and cross-genre film and fiction offer alternative ways of thinking about the relationship between Irish history and the Irish present that echo some aspects of cultural production in the 1916 period?

So let us return to that period, when – arguably – not only the foundations of the Irish state, but also the foundations of a literature which would interrogate that state, were beginning to be laid down. The year 1916 saw the publication of *A portrait of the artist as a young man*, in which James Joyce's alter ego Stephen famously vowed to 'fly by' the nets of nationality and religion. It is a statement that has usually been taken to imply an intention to escape or evade the twin shibboleths of early twentieth-century Irish nationalist sentiment, though it also carries the meaning of flying 'with the aid of' those beliefs. And precisely that combination of investment in and evasion of a national story characterizes the novel he was writing at the time *Portrait* was published. Let us consider three challenges to the national story laid down by *Ulysses*.

First, the question of history. One of the things we tend to forget about *Ulysses* is that it is a historical novel, albeit one about the very recent past. Joyce wrote it between 1914 and 1921, but the story is set at the turn of the century. Throughout the book there is a dynamic relationship between the ghosts of an Irish past (including, for example, Famine ghosts) and the present of 1904. But the present in which Joyce was writing also feeds back into the past of the novel. So for example Stephen imagines the boys in his history class slaughtered on a future battlefield, as the First World War casts a shadow over the story. How does contemporary art and culture develop this inheritance to figure the relationship between an Irish past and a global future?

Secondly, Joyce spent 1916, in Zurich, exploring Irish (and English) nationalism through the figure of an outsider, an assimilated Jew, a member of a race treated with suspicion and sometimes hatred. Through the Homeric and Jewish parallels the reader is asked to consider to what extent a nation is the same people living in the same place, 'and also in different places', as Leopold Bloom puts it. Joyce's ongoing challenge in *Ulysses* to think creatively about the boundaries of national identity has become only more pressing in light of the current refugee crisis. It is almost as though racial difference brackets a century of trying to forget about it. How are the boundaries of the nation figured in contemporary writing?

And lastly, Joyce's novel tells the story of Stephen's search for maturity as a search for a new and better family. His rejection of his ineffectual father and his refusal to kneel at the request of his dying mother are prerequisites for his encounter with Leopold Bloom, just as Bloom's exile from the family home is a necessary condition for his rapprochement with Stephen. While this alternative family romance may have been a productive way for Joyce to represent flying by the nets of church and state, has it become a trap for contemporary writers?

* * *

Let us begin with the family. Twentieth-century Irish fiction and drama have been heavily committed to presenting the family, and the dysfunctional family in particular, as a microcosm of the failure of the Irish state to nurture its people. The family home has functioned as a kind of shorthand for the alliance between church and state, in part because of the role of the priest as go-between, mediating between institutional and familial affairs. The metaphor has taken hold to such an extent that the family (and its cognate institution the school) often appears to stand in for church–state institutions. From popular dramatists such as John B. Keane and M.J. Molloy to Patrick Kavanagh, Samuel Beckett and novelists of the early 1960s such as Edna O'Brien and John McGahern, readers were confronted with parents who failed to nurture – parents who in effect starved and sold their children, or used them in other ways, as families became substitutes for and images of the state as inadequate parent. Mid-century Irish literature was full of plots that turned on the attempted rebellion of children and young people who were enslaved to an older generation, subjugated by parents who had been rendered at best passive, at worst instrumentalist in their attitudes to the young. This complex appeared not only in literary fiction, but popular drama and short stories, such as the gentle generational battles explored in the short fiction published in the popular family magazine *Ireland's Own*.

This popular familial-conflict plot was in fact a version of a plot that was central to the conception of the Rising itself (and indeed before the Rising stretching back to the Young Ireland movement). As the Proclamation declared, the revolutionaries were calling on men and women to act 'In the name of God and the dead generations.' The Rising was conceived in part as a commemoration – as an answer to or a re-enactment of a recurring need. The signatories to the Proclamation were declaring the duty owed to dead generations of revolutionaries to carry on the fight. But at the same time they were claiming strength for their own generation. A generation is a product of memory, but in this case it was also an aspiration – a product of the need to become the new generation, and in so doing to transform the debased present, in which the ideal of national sovereignty had been lost. The new generation needed to create itself as a generation by rejecting (at the very least seeing through) the failures of their parents, but at the same time the revolutionaries aspired to live up to a better version of the past.

The principal difference between Rising plots and, later, counter-revival and mid-century ones was not the rejection of dull or unimaginative or cruel parents, but the depressing realization that for all the sound and fury, heat and light, generated by political rebellion, the young were in much the same state as before, and now no political solution could be imagined. The solutions provided in mid-century texts were – again picking up on Joycean models – forms of disengagement rather than political engagement: emigration, retreat into language, rejections and refusals. And this trope of generational conflict is still shaping a great deal of contemporary fiction and drama – it is one of the legacies of 1916.

The mirror image of generational conflict is generational haunting, or the notion of an incomplete past – a past that because of its incompleteness keeps intruding into the present. The young who rebel against the older generation are attempting to end one story and start another, their own story, but the ghostly revisitings from the past suggest they cannot begin afresh. For Joyce writing *Ulysses* through the years of the Rising, the Anglo–Irish war and the civil war, the sense that the story of post-Parnellite Ireland was unfinished must have seemed self-evident. And it is not at all hard to find contemporary novels that engage, whether more or less explicitly, with the problem of a story that won't come to an end, a story whose effects spill out beyond the actors who are centrally involved in them.

A significant number of contemporary novels set in the recent past – Seamus Deane's *Reading in the dark*, Colm Tóibín's *Brooklyn* and *Nora*

Webster, Anne Enright's *The gathering* and *The green road*, Kevin Barry's *Beatlebone* – are stories written out of a fluid mixing of fictionalized personal memory and historical research. For that very reason, they are stories that stage the impact of past histories on the present, partly through the lingering of memory, but also in the dramatization of an incomplete past. Perhaps one of the clearest examples is *The gathering*, where Enright's narrator excavates an unfinished past of sexual abuse, which, as she slowly gathers, is still playing itself out in her own life and the lives of her siblings. In two separate scenes the narrator visits the (now abandoned) institution where her abused uncle was at one time incarcerated, and recalls a previous visit in her childhood, whose meaning she cannot exactly recover, but she can piece together, in the same way as she slowly pieces together the narrative of her brother's abuse.

Irish fiction and drama has always been ahead of the game in isolating hidden experiences of familial sexual abuse, or the collusion between the state and the church in perpetuating institutional regimes – consider the puritanical and destructive mother in Patrick Kavanagh's 'The Great Hunger', for example, the trace of the punishing religious institution in Beckett's 'Not I', or the figure of the paternal abuser in John McGahern's early fiction. For contemporary writers this tradition of the family as microcosm of the nation offers a strong model, although there may be a danger that stereotypes of inadequate parents, and especially bad mothers, are imported almost unconsciously along with it. And the number of monstrous or emotionally stunted mothers who crop up in contemporary Irish fiction is certainly noticeable. Even a novel as audacious and risk-taking as Eimear MacBride's *A girl is a half-formed thing* recycles the character of the inadequate, emotionally unresponsive mother. She appears in milder form in *The gathering*, in *Brooklyn*, and most recently in Emma Donoghue's absorbing novel *The wonder*. All these mothers are also victims, of course, but they are chiefly victimisers, and furthermore their lack of empathy, their willingness to sacrifice their children, derives from excessive religiosity. The alliance between mothers and the church – which we can trace all the way back to Stephen's mother in *Portrait* and *Ulysses* – overrules the needs of the young.

There is something troubling about the recurrence of this figure of the bad mother, who channels religious orthodoxies, or uses them as a defence, and arguably something strange about the persistence of the image of the puritanical mother figure in a period when the church itself has been in retreat. In the social realm recent revelations about mother-and-baby homes and industrial schools have drawn attention to the manner in which *both* mothers and children were sacrificed to an institutional regime that served the economic needs of the family as much as the moral requirements of the church. Thus we might contrast the portrayal of Irish motherhood in the film *Philomena* (which did very well at the box office) or indeed in Tóibín's *The testament of Mary*.

Part of the problem might be that fiction works with patterns that are hard to shift. There is a weight behind the familial national story that the writers cannot easily sidestep. Two recent novels, *The wonder* and *Nora Webster*, are intensely aware of the problems of using the family as a microcosm of the nation/state. Both are self-conscious about the debilitating effects of a repressed, hidden or secret past on the present, but they approach the issue in very different ways.

The wonder is set in the Irish midlands sometime in the late 1860s. We can think of it as a novel that wants to tell a story about generational haunting, but from the other end – from the perspective of post-Famine Ireland, when the haunting begins. It is a kind of mixed famine/anorexia story: the 'wonder' is a child who appears to have lived miraculously on nothing but prayer for months. The novel weaves together various genres. There is a romance plot, between the English ex-Nightingale nurse back from the Crimea and the journalist down from Dublin, who together form a sort of detective team, trying to establish whether the 9-year-old child is, in fact, being secretly fed by a member of her family. Rather like *The gathering*, the central female character, Lib, uncovers the narrative through her detective work. She is both story-maker and sleuth, like Mina Harker in *Dracula*. But she also serves – remember she is an English nurse – as scientific critic of the religious culture she encounters in Longford. There is a British-Irish opposition that is mapped on to an opposition between realism and superstition. What Lib uncovers is not what she is looking for, but instead a hidden story of incest and abuse, of which the miraculous starving child is collateral damage. And she uncovers an alliance between the local priest and the child's mother in keeping the abuse secret, even if it will destroy the child. What is striking about the novel is that while there are all sorts of Gothic, 'magical' elements to the grim family narrative Lib uncovers, Donoghue also chooses to resolve the framing love story with a fairy-tale, fantasy ending – the farmhouse is torched, allowing a new family (comprised of nurse, journalist, and rescued child) to be reborn out of the ashes. It is a version of *Jane Eyre*, set in small-farm, post-Famine Ireland, with an improbable ending in which the past really is wiped out – no haunting here – and the characters are able to create new lives for themselves, in Australia.

We can read this use of fairy tale as an attempt on Donoghue's part to break with the conventions of the realist plot, to find a way of acknowledging fantasy and wish-fulfilment as integral to the way the national story gets told (although arguably it does not disrupt the narrative of generational conflict I have been discussing). There is a comparable fairy-tale element in Tóibín's *Nora Webster*, a novel that admittedly appears to sit comfortably within the realist tradition. The narrative unfolds as a detailed, realistic account of the life of a widowed mother in a highly realised specific locale – Enniscorthy in the late 1960s (one hundred years after the story told in *The wonder*). Tóibín does a very good job of persuading his readers that they are safe in the world of narrative realism, but I would like to suggest that the novel's genre is not so easily determined. Yes, the novel is a portrait of a widowed mother, and it is certainly a bad-mother novel – but it is also a portrait, and the latest instalment in Tóibín's multi-volume biography, of a town. This is Enniscorthy on the cusp of, or in transition to, modernity. And in this seam of the story there are elements that sit rather oddly in a realist novel. Let us take Sister Thomas, for example – a character who materializes out of nowhere on several occasions, just as Nora needs help, and who appears not only to know all of everyone's history but to be able to sort out all possible problems if you entrust them to her. This is the nun as a good fairy, or representative from another world. Oddly enough, Edna O'Brien's recent novel *The little red chairs* also features a good-fairy nun, Sister Bonaventure, suggesting at the very least a pushback against the current social stereotype of nuns and women religious as unreflective conduits of a persecuting, moralistic church hierarchy. Yet another Gothic moment in Tóibín's novel occurs when Nora is visited by the ghost of her husband, a miraculous visitation that frees her to burn his letters (the literary material of her past) in the final pages of the novel.

These fairy and ghost elements are Tóibín's way of signalling the broader scope of history beyond the small town's obsessions with the social world of private liaisons, and the hierarchies of the golf club. (Is Nora's sister's new boyfriend a bank manager or does he just work in a bank?) But broader 'national' and historical questions are also signalled in a realist manner. The narrative traces a number of external forces that are beginning to make inroads on the town: trade unionism begins to challenge paternalistic family business; the more socially liberal world of Dublin starts to encroach on small-town conservatism; the big Dublin stores, so easily accessed by train, have an impact on local consumerism; and violence and civil disorder in Northern Ireland also make their impact felt. Civil rights, gun-running, Bloody Sunday, they all come to Enniscorthy through the television:

'Is this a film?' Conor asked.

'No, it's the news. It's Derry.'

The camera showed two or three of the marchers who had fallen to the ground, and then it followed some of the demonstrators who were running with the police in hot pursuit. The camera then focused on a woman who was screaming.

This scene takes place in the family front room. Nora and her sons watch the news along with Nora's brother-in-law and his wife. Following the scenes of violence in Derry the narrator's voice stays with Nora, who expects, reasonably enough, that there will be some discussion of what they have been watching. But nobody says anything and eventually she asks her brother-in-law what he thinks. He makes no comment apart from, 'That's one scrap I wouldn't like to be in. There will be no easy way out of that one.' As the unfolding crisis in Northern Ireland is covered by the television news the characters repeatedly turn their backs.

In the television-watching scenes Tóibín appears to acknowledge that a narrow and familial focus (a circumscribed, national focus) may be both a strength and a weakness. It is also worth noting that the critique is made manifest through generational conflict. The turn away from political crisis is not just the turning aside of the small town, but of the older generation. The Enniscorthy elders do not want to know, even when Nora's student daughter becomes involved in protests. They experience her unannounced appearance on the *Late Late Show* as an unwelcome disturbance of the safety of the sitting room.

If I am right about Tóibín's appraisal of an inward-looking society in the 1960s I think it may have some consequences for how we think about the current commemorations of 1916. And it also has consequences for the way that Irish literature and art have acknowledged a post-1916 story beyond the borders of the Republic. As though to emphasize this, Tóibín inserts into his novel a portrait of the artist, or rather an artist-documentarist of the real. Nora's eldest son Donal keeps pointing his camera lens at the television and taking pictures of the pictures – whether of the moon landing, or of the riots in Belfast and Derry. He is engaged in an artistic re-presentation of the real, a mathematical squaring of the power of the photograph to capture real life (as though in answer to Conor's question, he turns the news into film). His pictures may, or may not, be any good, but what they certainly are is unreadable. He spends hours in his dark room turning out images of haze, of indistinct shapes, of patches of light and dark. Is he transforming 'real life' into something meaningless, without clear boundaries, lacking the forms and

structures through which the real can be recognized? Or do his pictures
articulate the truth of the sitting room, as it were, the truth that in fact the
images of violence and the breakdown of order in Northern Ireland can't be
read or understood by people who are so far from that experience in the
South that they might as well be on the moon?

Donal performs the role of misunderstood artist so well in the novel
because it is so hard to distinguish it from the role of cranky teenager. He is
both inside and outside the contained world of his family, and his community
– an in-between position emphasized when he is ejected from the local hotel
for taking pictures of the moon landings on television. His intermediary
status is typical of the ethnographer, and in effect Tóibín reminds us through
Donal that his own perspective on the Enniscorthy of his youth is an
ethnographic one – an interpretation of a community for those who do not
belong to it, both in place and time, by one who knows it from both the inside
and the outside.

Both Donoghue and Tóibín deploy folkloric, Gothic and ethnographic
elements as means of putting pressure on the realist novel as a vehicle for the
story of the national community. Strands of fantasy, legend and documentary
can offer alternative forms of knowledge, other ways of remembering the
national story and what lies beyond the national frame. Of all these modes, I
wish to suggest, it is the ethnographic impulse that has proved most
productive for a variety of contemporary cultural practices that seek to
interrogate the stories the nation tells itself. To illustrate this I want to return
to the subject of migrants and outsiders, to the issue of racial difference that
I have suggested brackets a century of trying to forget about it.

The migrant has appeared in Irish literature throughout the twentieth
century primarily as an emigrant not an immigrant, and there are obvious
historical reasons for that. But I have been arguing that established literary
patterns, tropes, and plots can get in the way of thinking, as much as enable
it. And it may be that the focus on the emigrant has consequences for the
ability of contemporary literature to respond to the current migrant crisis. A
useful comparison here might be the way in which contemporary literature
and art tackles the environmental emergency which, like forced migration, is
both a global and a national emergency. The Indian novelist Amitav Ghosh
has recently argued that, apart from a few honourable exceptions (he
instances Cormac McCarthy and Margaret Atwood), contemporary novels
fail to represent climate catastrophe. His argument is similar to the one I am
making here, that the problem is not so much one of lack of information as
of novelistic form. Non-fiction, after all, finds methods of examining the
manner in which humans have become geological agents, changing the most

basic physical process of the Earth. But the novel, says Ghosh, is engaged in masking conditions as much as unmasking them. His argument depends on the idea that the narrativity of life – the idea that an individual or group of individuals' life stories can be told at all – depends on foregrounding everyday details, and crucially on accounting for existence on an individual scale. In the context of global environmental forces, '[t]he irony of the "realist" novel, the very gestures with which it conjures up reality are actually a concealment of the real'.[3] I would like to go further and suggest that precisely because the novel developed as a means of telling national stories through individual (or familial) ones, it ends up concealing, rather than revealing, the forces shaping contemporary globalized existence. What happens when lives cannot be narrated according to national plots – even plots in which people travel about a lot? Like the politics of the carbon economy, the experiences of migrants, asylum seekers and refugees are currently being addressed by political and legal activists, but less so by writers and artists. It is no accident that the few contemporary Irish counter-examples are also works that engage deeply with the formal problems of telling 'national' stories.

Take the work of ANU Productions, and particularly the series of plays produced as the Monto Cycle, the last of which (*Vardo*) focuses on Eastern European sex workers trafficked into Ireland. Director Louise Lowe has explained that the Monto works were born of an attempt to think through 'what it meant to look at our state in microcosm, and how we would investigate and interrogate what had happened to us as a society within a very tiny community, but also then I suppose as a state'. Rather than the family as microcosm of the state, the focus in the Monto Cycle is on place, and community, and the social institutions that have helped define them across time. And as part of the process of developing the works, access to the community was gained through explicitly ethnographic methods: lengthy interviews and oral histories that complemented historical research. In fact Lowe's own position as 'author' or arranger of the works who also has personal links with the community arguably mirrors Tóibín's insider-outsider status in relation to Enniscorthy.

Ethnography, the collecting of tales and stories, documentary, and explorations of personal memory – these procedures lie at the heart of much of the most interesting contemporary work that asks us to reflect on the nature of historical knowledge. In fact ethnographic artworks offer an often self-conscious alternative to broader national histories by concentrating on

3 A. Ghosh, *The great derangement: climate change and the unthinkable* (Chicago, 2016), p. 23.

inescapably local memory, and exploring particular landscapes and social environments that are saturated with shared associations.[4] As the work of ANU Productions insists, these memories are never pure or unmediated – they get reinvented at multiple points in response to events (including commemorative events). And precisely because they are open-ended, memory and storytelling offer a means of undermining the idea that the past is history, that the past is over. Site-specific works bring past and present together in dynamic relationship, as the audience and actors move back and forth between the 'now' of the performance space, and the 'then' of the historical space.[5]

Vardo is a performance piece that insists on migrants as subjects – rather than sources of pity or stereotypes of otherness. The stories into which audience members are introduced as participants are derived from the stories of migrant women gathered during ethnographic and oral-history research. Comparable contemporary works that also attend to migrant experience include the documentary films directed by Alan Grossman and Áine O'Brien of the Centre for Transcultural Research and Media Practice. *Here to stay* (2006) and *Promise and unrest* (2010) both focus on the Filipino community in Dublin, the first exploring the political and trade union activism of a male nurse who is also a drag performance artist, and the second the back-and-forth relationship between a mother and daughter living family life across the distance between Ireland and the Philippines. The films were made over spans of four and five years, respectively, and they explore two national-global locales, tied by travel and the telephone, as well as income. Arguably nothing could be more different than these films and the site-specific works I've mentioned. ANU's performances are determinedly local; they cannot be duplicated, or internationalized in any easy sense. Grossman and O'Brien's documentaries, on the other hand, can be played on any laptop with a DVD slot, anywhere in the world. But what these works share is the ethnographic impulse – they are all self-conscious attempts to remember and acknowledge a community through its stories. Grossman has written persuasively about his search for an artistic means of generating empathy, more than, or in addition to, a sympathetic account of the problems of the others with whom we live in what Judith Butler calls 'unwilled adjacency', a state in which human subjects are 'already given over from the start to a world of others'.[6]

---

4 A comparable example in the visual arts is the work of Dorothy Cross. See in particular *Ghost ship* (1999) and *Chiasm* (1999); for a discussion of Cross' site-specific works, see R. Lydenberg, *Gone: site-specific works by Dorothy Cross* (Chestnut Hill, MA, 2005).   5 For a discussion of this aspect of the work see B. Singleton, *ANU Productions: the Monto Cycle* (London, 2016).   6 A. Grossman, 'Curiously mediating identity formations across

What I want to focus on here is Grossman's conviction that the work he is producing is ethnography, not fiction, and that it has to be, in order to generate the kind of open-ended structures that can allow us as viewers to travel between the here of Ireland and the there of the Philippines, and to begin to deconstruct that opposition.

This is not, then, an argument for a particular type of content. The dangers of importing migrant 'voices' into works that make no formal concessions to globalized life stories are apparent in Edna O'Brien's ambitious recent novel *The little red chairs*, an audacious counter-history of Bosnian war criminal Radovan Karadzic on the run in the West of Ireland. Karadzic is thinly disguised in the novel, but was apparently so well disguised in real life that he was able to evade capture by trading openly in Belgrade and Vienna as Dr Dragan David Dabic, peddler of alternative medicine and intense pseudo-Romantic lyric poetry. O'Brien's plot, which involves a romantic liaison between Dragan and a local woman (Fidelma), dissolves any comfortable boundary between the nice people of Sligo and the nasty history of Serbia. Contemporary Ireland is implicated in the fratricidal violence of Eastern Europe; later in the novel it is implicated in the effects of the war on terror. Fidelma seeks refuge in London, where she lives on the margins with desperate refugees from other wars, from domestic slavery, and sexual and physical abuse, for whom London's anonymous twilight economy is a last hope. Fidelma's precarious status as both victim and perpetrator (because she has taken Dragan as her lover) allows O'Brien to explore questions of responsibility and collusion, and the extent to which comfortable living in the West depends on discomfort, murder and torture elsewhere. The book is full of harrowing testimonies, from the displaced in London, and from the Bosnian victims of Dragan/Karadzic who Fidelma encounters when she travels to The Hague to witness his trial. Through Fidelma, O'Brien asks us not only not to look away from the kind of atrocities that are rarely addressed in contemporary Irish fiction, or indeed in much contemporary Irish political discourse either; she asks us to consider the ways in which we collude in them.

Yet the narrative structure of the novel undermines its purpose, as what are in effect migrant witness testimonies are subordinated to the central narrative. A significant portion of the novel is given over to monologues, through which migrants and others tell their stories. So the migrants who work in the kitchens of the local hotel each tell a tale in turn, unfortunately mostly in present-tense foreigner-speak ('Then war happen. My family they

borders and interdisciplinary boundaries: transcultural film practice', in *Transcultural identity constructions in a changing world* (Frankfurt, 2016), p. 35.

lose everything …'; 'Place very lonely. Only cows and shed where I sleep.');
the displaced who meet in the refugee centre in London recount their
experiences of violation as a form of expiation. But despite the different
accents in which these stories are spoken, they remain curiously flat and
undifferentiated, indeed curiously lacking in an imagined interior life. It is as
though nothing is hidden in the stories we tell of ourselves, and that the work
of literature is to present them as straightforwardly as possible. There is
clearly a valuable humanitarian impulse behind O'Brien's collection and
presentation of migrant and refugee tales, but in this novel the stories fail to
provide more than local colour. To use Grossman's formulation, they elicit
the reader's sympathy, rather than her empathy.

I have been suggesting that contemporary literary and art practice has
been productively fractured or pluralized in ways that may mirror Joyce's
turn-of-the-twentieth-century Ireland: site-specific performances that
require audience members to import their own present experience and their
own memories into Ireland's past; the work of documentary makers and
multi-media practitioners who are telling the stories of today's migrants and
disturbing the time and teleology of migration along with the boundaries
between here and elsewhere. It may be too much to suggest that today's
interest in local stories and tales may hark back to, or echo, a similar interest
in local experience that animated art and literature in the years leading up to
the Rising (such as the work of Augusta Gregory, or Jeremiah Curtin, for
example). However, one recent mixed-media work does make the link
explicit. Donnacha Dennehy's recent opera *Hunger*, a collaboration with Iarla
Ó Lionáird, revisits the diary of the Famine years written by American
traveller and ethnographer Asenath Nicholson, combining Nicholson's text
with fragments of other art forms (classical music, poetry, folklore and
traditional Irish song) and interviews with contemporary economists and
historians discussing past and present famines.[7] It is an uncompromisingly
multi-layered and open-ended performance piece in which past and present
ethnographies, and theories of political science and economy interrogate one
another through the medium of music.

I would like to end with some thoughts on ethnographers as interpreters
of stories – and my emphasis here is again on the fact that stories conceal as
much as they reveal. In a recent essay on Famine folklore Angela Bourke
draws subtle distinctions between what she calls stories that remember and
stories that forget the Famine. She argues for the need to interpret legend

---

7 M. Keegan-Dolan's *Swan Lake / Loch na hEala* (2016) offers a comparable mix of
storytelling, folklore, and traditional and classical music.

and folklore – local storytelling – as a form of 'vernacular magical realism', a kind of Gothic or ghostly translation of real historical and economic crisis into another shape. She claims, for example, that the burgeoning mid-nineteenth-century genre of stories of malevolent people from another world must be interpreted in the context of social pressures, in particular the pressure that the Famine put on a local moral economy of co-operation and mutual aid. The impossible choices that people were forced to make, between refusing to help others, or failing to protect their own communities, could only be addressed indirectly:

> Thousands of these oral belief-legends concern strangers who lurk on the edges of a community and make demands, exacting revenge when refused, or rewarding those who help them. Storytellers identify the strangers obliquely, in terms that mark them as fundamentally different from 'us'. They do not describe them as starving refugees ...[8]

The refugees seem to have been 'forgotten' in much Famine folklore. They have been buried in the process of storytelling, yet they appear once we know how to read for them. It is precisely this skill – the ability to read for and uncover the implicit meanings in the stories people tell – that distinguishes the writers and artists I have been discussing today. If we are to keep challenging the outwardly straightforward stories a nation likes to tell itself, we need to look to the ethnographers, interpreters and translators of those stories, in other words to the novelists, poets, film-makers, composers, dramatists and artists who, like Donal in *Nora Webster*, deform real-life stories in order to re-form them through artistic practice, and reveal their hidden elements. I have been exploring the ways in which contemporary writers engage with inherited genres, and tropes such as unfinished histories, migrants and refugees, and the family as microcosm of the state. But beyond particular genres and themes it is the confidence and concentration with which Irish writers and artists continue to interrogate narratives of the nation that is the principle cultural legacy of 1916.

8 A. Bourke, *Voices underfoot: memory, forgetting and oral verbal art* (Hamden, CT, 2016), p. 32.

Independent Ireland in comparative perspective[1]

KEVIN HJORTSHØJ O'ROURKE

Somebody clever, I'm not sure who, is supposed to have once said that 'he who only tries to understand Ireland will not even understand Ireland'. There can at times be an attention-seeking particularism about Irish writing – look at us, we like to say, mostly to ourselves, but if possible to any foreigners who might be listening as well – look at us, and at how unique, and at how very interesting we are.

When I was a young boy in primary school, we were taught that post-independence Ireland was poor but uniquely virtuous. Today, we are taught that it was poor and uniquely wicked. Both positions are misguided: we were never as different as people have made out. Those traditional rural values that we once correctly celebrated can still be found in agricultural communities around the world; *meitheal* is not a uniquely Irish phenomenon. And the Magdalene Laundries that we now correctly condemn have their counterparts elsewhere as well.[2] The past, it turns out, is a foreign country everywhere.

And what is true of Irish social history turns out to be true of Irish economic history as well. Very often, the things that were happening in Ireland at a particular time were in fact part of a bigger, European, or even global story.

I used to think that the quotation with which I started this paper was due to Nicholas Canny, whose own work has largely been concerned with placing the history of early modern Ireland into the context of the wider world – but he denies it.

1 This is a revised version of a lecture delivered on 11 Nov. 2016 at the conference 'Ireland 1916–2016: the promise and challenge of national sovereignty'. I am extremely grateful to Nicholas Canny for having invited me; to everyone at NUIG for their hospitality; to John McHale for chairing the session so expertly, and to the discussants for their excellent comments. I am also grateful to Brian Ashcroft, Frank Barry, Jason Begley, George Boyer, Alan de Bromhead, Graham Brownlow, Diane Coyle, Richard Dorsett, Alan Fernihough, James Foreman-Peck, Frank Geary, Stefanie Haller, David Jordan, Aidan Kane, Michael Keating, Morgan Kelly, Dave Madden, Maurice Mulcahy, Cormac Ó Gráda, Eunan O'Halpin, Andy O'Rourke, Martin Sandbu, and Rebecca Stuart, for many helpful comments, advice, data and technical assistance. The usual disclaimer applies. 2 On Denmark, see J. Adler-Olsen, *Guilt* (London, 2014).

On the other hand, I am quite certain that it was Rudyard Kipling who once asked 'what they know of England who only England know?' It seems as though the temptation to focus on one's own country, and to ignore what was going on around it, is not just an Irish phenomenon – which of course merely reinforces the point that we are not as unique as we sometimes think we are.

My main purpose in this paper is therefore to place Ireland's post-independence economic history into some sort of comparative context, and to try to convince you that in fact our economic history is in many respects not all that unusual.

The circumstances of our state's birth were of course dramatic, and for a while we held the world's attention; but then we settled down to become what we had chosen to become: a small, rather poor country on the periphery of Europe. In many ways, I'm going to argue, our subsequent economic history is precisely what you would have predicted, given the turn that twentieth-century European history was about to take. Our economic *policies* were not that unusual in the context of the time; and over the long run our economic *performance* was just about exactly what you would have predicted as well.

But this volume is being published under the shadow of Brexit, and the question that arises is: will Boris and his merry band of Brexiteers succeed in finishing the job that was begun in 1916, and complete the economic and political separation between our island and Great Britain? Will their efforts lead to Ireland becoming more fully independent of Britain than it has been to date, and perhaps uncomfortably so? Will we have to stand more squarely on our own two feet than we might perhaps want?

And so a second major theme here will be Ireland's economic relationships over the course of the last century with both Britain and continental Europe. If there is one way in which our post-independence economic history was indeed unusual for many decades, and unhelpfully so, it was our excessive dependence on a poorly performing British economy. Membership of the European Communities in 1973, and the European single-market programme of the late 1980s and early 1990s, were absolutely crucial in transforming Ireland's fortunes.

THE NINETEENTH-CENTURY BACKSTORY

It doesn't make sense to discuss Ireland's post-independence economic performance without spending at least some time on the colonial backstory. Irish economic performance under British rule was disappointing, and occasionally tragic. The Famine of the 1840s was genuinely unusual – the last

mass subsistence crisis in peacetime Western Europe, with the exception of
the Finnish famine of the 1860s. As we all know, it ushered in a wave of mass
emigration that persisted into the twentieth century, and that led to the quite
unique spectacle of a continuously declining population throughout the late
nineteenth century, a time when Europe as a whole was experiencing a
population explosion.

4.1 Gross decadal emigration rates per 1,000

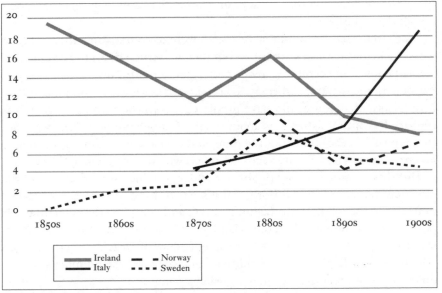

Source: Hatton and Williamson (1994, p. 536), cited in note 3.

Even here, however, we have to be careful not to overdo the peculiarity of
the Irish experience. By the end of the period, Italy was experiencing
emigration rates well in excess of our own, with Norway also experiencing
heavy outflows (see figure 4.1).[3] Furthermore, the same underlying forces
were driving emigration throughout Europe during this period. Emigration
rates were systematically higher in: countries with higher birth rates;
countries that were poorer; and countries with a prior history of emigration.[4]
Ireland's marital fertility rate was high; the country was very poor; and the
Famine had resulted in an extremely high stock of Irish people living
overseas, and particularly in North America. High emigration rates are

3 T.J. Hatton & J.G. Williamson, 'What drove the mass migrations from Europe in the late
nineteenth century?', *Population and Development Review*, 20 (1994), 533–59.   4 T.J. Hatton
& J.G. Williamson, *The age of mass migration: causes and economic impact* (New York, 1998).

exactly what you would have expected in the circumstances; there is no need to appeal to any supposed peculiarities of the Irish psyche in order to explain our high propensity to leave the country during the period.[5]

This nineteenth-century economic history had important consequences for the twentieth century. I want to highlight three legacies in particular.

First: since a history of previous emigration leads to a higher tendency to emigrate in the future, Irish people remained extremely mobile after independence. Indeed, the population of the twenty-six counties continued to decline until 1961. Emigration could be both beneficial and harmful to the economy, in ways that generations of Irish economists, politicians and historians have discussed over the years.

One consequence was that by lowering the domestic supply of labour, Irish emigration raised Irish wages, pulling them up towards the levels available on labour markets overseas. Something very similar happened in both Norway and Italy.[6] On the one hand, this helped sustain living standards that would otherwise not have been attainable; but on the other, it deprived the economy to at least some extent of one of the main advantages that poor countries generally possess, namely cheap labour.

On the eve of the First World War, Ireland was still poor, but it was clearly much richer than it had been in the 1870s, let alone the 1840s. But growth in per-capita living standards that was largely due to a declining population was hardly anything to shout about. Southern Ireland's prosperity in 1913, such as it was, was based on very different foundations than prosperity elsewhere. The key to economic growth during the late nineteenth century was typically industrialization. And the key to industrialization, in Germany, Italy, France, the United States, and elsewhere, was protectionism.

During the late twentieth and early twenty-first centuries, globalization and growth have gone hand in hand, but tariffs protecting industry were strongly and positively correlated with growth before the First World War.[7] As a region of the free-trading United Kingdom, an independent tariff policy was obviously unavailable to Ireland. The data plotted in figure 4.2 show that nationalists were not mad, in the context of the time, to believe that this was a serious handicap. And so a second legacy of the nineteenth century, which became important in the twentieth century, was an ideological commitment

5 An excellent discussion of nineteenth-century Irish demography is provided in T. Guinnane, *The vanishing Irish: households, migration, and the rural economy in Ireland, 1850–1914* (Princeton, 1997).   6 K.H. O'Rourke & J.G. Williamson, *Globalization and history: the evolution of a nineteenth-century Atlantic economy* (Cambridge, MA, 1999), ch. 8. 7 S.H. Lehmann & K.H. O'Rourke, 'The structure of protection and growth in the late nineteenth century', *Review of Economics and Statistics*, 93 (2010), 606–16.

to protectionism among a certain stratum of Irish nationalist thinkers. Once again, there was nothing unusual about this; it was rather the United Kingdom, with its strong commitment to more or less unilateral free trade, even as its rivals gained market share at its expense, which was the exception during this period.

4.2 Manufacturing tariffs versus growth, 1875–1913

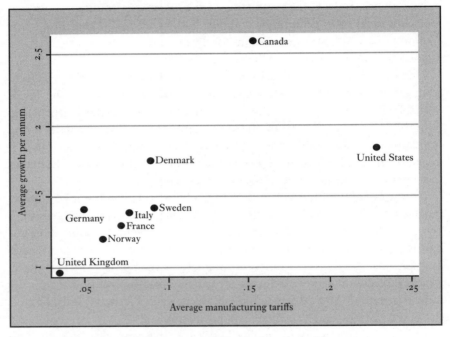

Source: Based on data in Lehmann and O'Rourke (2010) cited in note 7.

But this intellectual commitment to protectionism would eventually run up against a third legacy of Ireland's history, which was the extent to which the Irish and British economies were intertwined. The south of Ireland was overwhelmingly specialized in agricultural activities, and its agricultural exports went overwhelmingly to the United Kingdom. The Irish and British labour markets were very tightly integrated with each other. The Irish Free State, and later the Irish Republic, would share a common legal system with Britain, as well as a common currency, and many other institutions. For much of the twentieth century it makes sense to regard Ireland as one small regional component of a broader British and Irish economy. And the problem was that this broader British and Irish economy, within which the British component was obviously overwhelmingly dominant, was a poor performer within the broader European context. Only when we emancipated ourselves from excessive reliance on our nearest neighbour were we able to finally grow as rapidly as other poor countries around the European periphery.

ASSESSING IRISH PERFORMANCE

In order to assess Ireland's economic performance, we need a benchmark.[8] Because of our history, a natural tendency is to use the UK, but that is an important mistake. The UK performed poorly relative to most European economies: by using it as a benchmark, we are setting the bar much too low.

A second alternative is to compare Ireland with similar regions inside the UK – Northern Ireland most obviously, but perhaps also Scotland and

4.3 Initial income and subsequent growth, 1926–2001

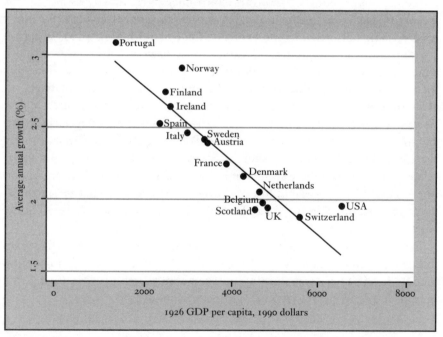

Source: Broadberry and Klein (2012) cited note 9. GNP rather than GDP is used for Ireland, using adjustment ratios kindly provided by Rebecca Stuart. Her data go back to 1944 so I have simply assumed that GNP was the same proportion of GDP in previous years, cited in note 8.

8 For a similar discussion, see C. Ó Gráda, *A rocky road: the Irish economy since the 1920s* (Manchester, 1997).

Wales. As we will see, doing so provides us with several useful insights, but again, by comparing ourselves with regions located within the slowly growing UK economy, we are setting the bar too low.

A third alternative, which makes a lot more sense, is to compare ourselves with other relatively poor economies around the European periphery. Greece, Portugal and Spain were all as poor as Ireland at the start of the twentieth century, if not poorer. They therefore faced many of the same obstacles that we did, but they also shared the same potential for rapid growth based on catching up on the industrial core. How did we do compared with these economies? Indeed, how did we do compared with European economies more generally?

It is a matter of statistical fact that within Western Europe, countries that were initially poorer have grown more rapidly than countries that were initially richer during the twentieth century. In other words, poorer economies have tended to converge on richer ones, mostly as a result of importing best-practice technologies already adopted elsewhere. We don't have reliable national-income evidence for Ireland before 1926, so figure 4.3 plots initial income levels, per capita, in 1926, against average growth per annum over the course of the subsequent seventy-five years.[9] I have done this for the broadest available sample of European countries that managed to avoid becoming communist later in the century, as well as the United States. As can be seen, there is a very clear negative relationship between these two variables. Initially poor countries, such as Portugal, grew much more rapidly than initially rich countries such as Switzerland. The average statistical relationship between these two variables (what economists call 'the regression line') is given by the straight line in the figure. As can be seen, the 'statistical fit' of this relationship is remarkably tight, in that countries are very closely clustered around this line.

Strikingly, Ireland's economic performance during the seventy-five years following 1926 was *exactly* what it should have been, given Ireland's initial income level. There was nothing unusual about Irish growth during this period. It was an entirely typical European economy.

THE INTERWAR PERIOD AND THE SECOND WORLD WAR: 1922–50

If there is one thing that is unusual about Irish economic policymaking after independence, it is that it took so long for the Irish Free State to move in a

9 S. Broadberry & A. Klein, 'Aggregate and per capita GDP in Europe, 1870–2000: Continental, regional and national data with changing boundaries', *Scandinavian*

protectionist direction. The successor states of the Austro–Hungarian empire, for example, immediately implemented a wide range of protectionist measures. By contrast, during the first ten years of Irish independence our trade policy was, comparatively speaking, remarkably liberal.

As we all know, the election of Fianna Fáil in 1932 coincided with a dramatic shift towards protection. But there are three questions about this policy shift that we can usefully ask. First, are its causes really to be found in Irish party politics alone? Second, was Ireland unusually protectionist? And third, was Irish protectionism unusually costly?

Regarding the first question: it would be a mistake to view the switch to protection as having had causes that were fundamentally idiosyncratic and Irish. *Everybody* switched towards protection following the onset of the Great Depression in 1929. Even the traditionally free-trading British moved decisively towards protection in November 1931 and February 1932 – that is to say, before Ireland.

This common trend requires a common explanation, which is provided by the Great Depression. The Great Depression arose from a catastrophic macroeconomic policy failure, largely associated with the gold standard of the period. This ruled out the sorts of loose-money policies that have been used in many economies during our own Great Recession, and was associated with an extremely conservative mindset when it came to fiscal policy as well. Governments thus found themselves unable to combat falling output and rising unemployment using the sorts of measures that Keynes was advocating at the time; with their hands thus tied behind their backs, they resorted to the only policy lever available to them, namely protection.[10] The hope was that this would create domestic jobs by shielding the local economy from import competition, and in fact in many cases, including our own, it did so. On average, higher tariffs were associated with better economic performance during the interwar period, other things being equal.[11] From a collective point of view of course, it would have been far preferable for everyone to have adopted coordinated and expansionary macroeconomic policies, as was done in 2009, and for them to have maintained relatively free international trading conditions. But this is not what happened, and it would be wrong to single out Ireland for special criticism in this regard.

Economic History Review, 60 (2012), 79–107.   10 B. Eichengreen & D.A. Irwin, 'The slide to protectionism in the Great Depression: who succumbed and why?', *Journal of Economic History*, 70 (2010), 871–97.   11 M. Clemens & J. Williamson, 'Why did the tariff–growth correlation change after 1950?', *Journal of Economic Growth*, 9 (2004), 5–46.

4.4 Was Ireland unusually protectionist? Average tariffs, 1922–38

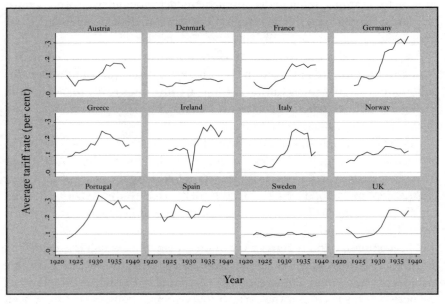

Source: Clemens and Williamson (2004) and www.duanaire.ie at NUI Galway, cited in note 11.

Was Ireland unusually protectionist during the 1930s? The answer is no. Irish average tariffs were towards the higher end of the spectrum in the sample of European countries for which we have data, but they were similar to those in Germany, Italy, Portugal, Spain and the UK (see figure 4.4). But focusing on tariffs alone is misleading, since these were not the real problem during the 1930s. Rather, countries during this period adopted a wide variety of quantitative restrictions on trade, up to and including exchange controls that in some cases effectively nationalized the international trading activities of particular countries. Ireland didn't do anything nearly as drastic. And as can be seen from figure 4.5,[12] it was towards the more liberal end of the spectrum when it came to the adoption of quotas as well.

Another well-known feature of Irish economic policy during this period was its attempts to restrict the foreign ownership of Ireland-based firms. But the importance and uniqueness of the 1932 and 1934 Control of Manufacturers Acts can be overdone. First, as work by Mary Daly, Frank

12 League of Nations, *Quantitative trade controls: their causes and nature* (Geneva, 1943); C.R. Whittlesey, 'Import quotas in the United States', *Quarterly Journal of Economics*, 52 (1937), 37–65.

4.5 How unusual was Irish trade policy? Percentage of imports covered by quantitative restrictions, 1937

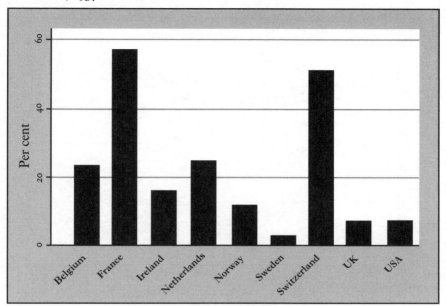

Source: League of Nations (1943), Whittlesey (1937) cited in note 12.

Barry, and others has revealed, these formal restrictions were often evaded by means of fancy legal footwork, as indeed was the case in other countries during this period.[13] Second, Ireland was by no means alone in adopting such restrictions. Spain restricted the foreign ownership and management of all firms to a maximum of 25 per cent in 1939.[14] In the same year, Finland tightened its existing restrictions on inward foreign investment, prohibiting the acquisition of real estate by foreign individuals, organizations, and Finnish companies that did not restrict foreign ownership to a maximum of 20 per cent of the outstanding shares.[15] Portugal restricted inward investment in 1943.[16] Other examples could be found.

13 M.E. Daly, 'An Irish-Ireland for business? The Control of Manufactures Acts, 1932 and 1934', *Irish Historical Studies*, 24 (1984), 246–72. M.E. Daly, *Industrial development and Irish national identity, 1922–1939* (New York, 1992). F. Barry, L. Barry & A. Menton, 'Tariff-jumping foreign direct investment in protectionist era Ireland', *Economic History Review*, 69 (2016), 1285–1308. 14 S. Lieberman, *The contemporary Spanish economy: a historical perspective* (London, 2006), p. 131. 15 R. Hjerppe, 'The significance of foreign direct investment in a small industrializing economy: the case of Finland in the interwar period', *Business and Economic History On-Line*, 1 (2004), 1–21 at 4–5. 16 J.L.C. das Neves, 'Portuguese postwar growth: a global approach' in N. Crafts & G. Toniolo (eds), *Economic growth in Europe since 1945* (Cambridge, 1996), pp 329–54 at p. 331.

4.6 Initial income and subsequent growth, 1926–38

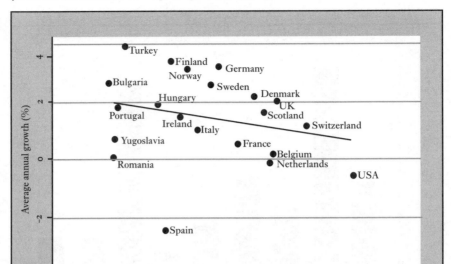

Source: as for figure 4.3.

Were the economic effects of protectionism uniquely destructive in Ireland? Again, the answer is no. As figure 4.6 shows, not only were Ireland's economic *policies* typical during this period, so was its economic *performance*. Between 1926 and 1938, Ireland grew at *exactly* the rate that it should have done, given its initial starting point.

Importantly, protectionism probably helped maintain employment at a time when jobs were scarce everywhere. It is true that the economic war with Britain, which lasted from 1932 to 1938, was somewhat unusual – although Ireland was hardly alone in defaulting on its debts during this period. But it is also true that the dispute was settled on terms highly favourable to the Irish. A capitalized £100 million liability was settled with a £10 million lump-sum payment, and Ireland gained the Treaty Ports into the bargain. This surely helped the country to remain neutral during the Second World War. Neutrality certainly saved many Irish lives, and it is entirely possible that it avoided much destruction to Irish property. Even taking the undoubted costs of the economic war into account, it is entirely plausible that its net economic impact was actually beneficial.[17]

17 J.P. Neary & C. Ó Gráda, 'Protection, economic war and structural change: the 1930s

The war itself was a very difficult period for the Irish economy, even though we were spared the horrors of the fighting. Imports of energy and other essential requirements were very scarce; domestic industry suffered accordingly. As a predominantly agricultural economy, with no heavy industry to speak of, the Irish Free State did not benefit from the demand for war-related matériel in the way that Scotland and Northern Ireland did. Even worse, it found itself selling its agricultural output to a hard-pressed British customer, which quite understandably used its monopoly position to lower the prices it paid for Irish agricultural produce. Even still, Irish farmers were the only section of the community to see their living standards rise between 1939 and 1943.[18]

In common with almost all of Western Europe, Ireland experienced a strong boom between 1945 and 1950. In formerly belligerent powers, especially on the Continent, the boom largely took the form of reconstruction. In the Irish case, it was far more consumption-driven, as consumers made up for lost time and bought American and other imported goods. Construction also boomed, as did industry.[19] Such a consumption-driven boom was probably less sustainable than the more investment-based booms experienced in continental Europe at the time. Nevertheless, the overall impression that one gets when placing Irish economic policies between 1922 and 1950 into a comparative perspective is that there was nothing unusually perverse or self-destructive about Irish policy choices during this period. Irish politicians were relatively liberal during the 1920s, and were protectionist like everybody else from 1932 onwards. They were hardly to blame for the deprivations of the Second World War, nor could they be praised for the inevitable recovery that followed. And the country's economic performance during the first thirty years of independence was also pretty typical for the time.

IRELAND FALLS BEHIND: 1950–73

In contrast, Ireland's performance during the subsequent twenty-five years was disappointing. Whereas Ireland had been an average performer during the dismal interwar period, it performed well below average during Europe's 'golden age'. The 1950s were as we all know particularly bad, and the GNP data plotted for Ireland in panel A of figure 4.7 understate the case, if it is the

in Ireland', *Irish Historical Studies*, 27 (1991), 250–66. K. O'Rourke, 'Burn everything British but their coal: the Anglo-Irish economic war of the 1930s', *Journal of Economic History*, 51 (1991), 357–66. **18** Ó Gráda, *A rocky road*, pp 7–21. **19** Ibid., pp 21–5.

4.7 Initial income and subsequent growth, 1950–60 and 1960–73

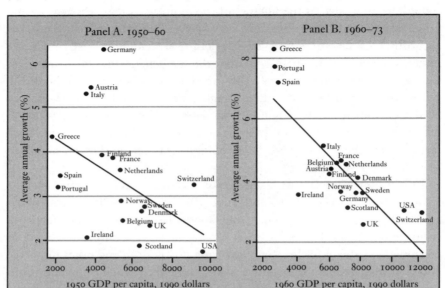

Source: as for figure 4.3.

living standards of ordinary people that we are concerned with. Throughout post-war Europe, governments erected modern welfare states, but Ireland lagged far behind. If independent Ireland can be said to have 'failed' during any period, it did so most obviously during this decade.

What may come as more of a surprise is the fact that Irish under-performance continued during the 1960s. As can be seen from panel B of figure 4.7, this was the decade during which Greece, Portugal and Spain experienced their economic miracles. Ireland, by contrast, was still an underperformer. Importantly, a comparison with Britain alone would miss this: from 1960 onwards the Irish economy grew more rapidly than the British one. But growing more rapidly than an economy which was itself an underachiever was not enough to prevent Ireland from falling even further behind mainstream Europe.

Why was Ireland's performance so poor during these two crucial decades? I want to highlight three reasons. The first has to do with recurrent balance-of-payments crises; the second has to do with delayed liberalization; and the third has to do with our excessive dependence on the poorly performing British economy.

The first feature of the Irish economy during the 1950s and early 1960s, which was obvious to people at the time but is less often commented upon today, was the succession of booms and busts.[20] The post-war boom ended as a result of a balance-of-payments crisis that emerged in 1950, and got worse in 1951. This ultimately led to the highly deflationary budget of April 1952, which caused a deep recession. By 1955 the economy was recovering, consumption was booming, and imports were rising rapidly. Once again, the eventual response was not one, but two austerity budgets in 1956, leading to a deep recession lasting several years. Ten years later, a rising trade deficit in 1965 was followed by yet another deflationary budget in 1966. This succession of booms and busts was highly destructive. It also poses the question of whether Irish policymakers were uniquely incompetent.

As it happens, they were not. This sequence of loosening fiscal policy, leading to rising incomes, rising imports, balance-of-payments crises, and thence to tightening fiscal policy, falling incomes, falling imports, and improvements in the balance of payments, was well-known in the United Kingdom and other countries at this time. The UK, for example, experienced major crises in 1957, 1961 and 1966. The term that we use to describe this sequence of events is 'stop-go policies', and the fundamental reasons for such policies were analysed by an Australian economist, Trevor Swan, in a famous and influential contribution to the macroeconomic literature.[21] The essential problem, Swan pointed out, was that governments of the time were trying to hit two targets simultaneously, a full-employment target and a trade-balance target. To hit two targets, you need at least two policy instruments; the problem was that during this period policymakers only had one, namely fiscal policy. The post-war Bretton Woods system was based on fixed exchange rates. These were supposed to be adjustable, and indeed they were occasionally adjusted, but to devalue your currency was seen as failure by politicians, and generally only happened under duress, in the context of major crises such as the one in 1967 that forced Harold Wilson to devalue the British, and thus the Irish, pound.

This implied a major dilemma for countries with currencies that were overvalued. Since their goods were overpriced on international markets, they faced persistent balance-of-trade problems. These could be overcome by tightening fiscal policy, which would lower expenditure and hence imports, but that came at the cost of higher unemployment. When unemployment

20 One notable exception is Ó Gráda, *A rocky road*, on which I draw extensively in the account below.   21 Arndt (1976) provides a detailed account of the genesis of the idea. H.W. Arndt, 'Non-traded goods and the balance of payments: the Australian contribution', *Economic Record*, 52 (1976), 104–7.

became too burdensome, fiscal policy could be loosened again, but this would imply rising trade deficits. The ultimate solution was to devalue the currency; until this happened, stop-go policies would be inevitable. And whereas devaluation was an option for the United Kingdom, it was not something that Irish policymakers could do unilaterally – so long as they were unwilling to break the Irish currency's link with sterling. Until then, booms and busts related to balance-of-payments crises were unsurprising – and indeed, British and Irish booms and busts were highly correlated with each other during this period.[22]

A second explanation for poor Irish performance during the European golden age, and particularly during the 1950s, is the delay in reversing interwar protectionist policies. I have argued that these policies were appropriate in the context of the 1930s, a time when everyone was protecting their domestic markets; when an export-oriented growth strategy was therefore not feasible; and when jobs were scarce everywhere. But by the 1950s protectionism was clearly no longer appropriate. At the urgent behest of the United States, European countries were gradually removing barriers to trade and integrating their economies with each other – first within the context of the Organization for European Economic Co-operation, the forerunner of today's Organization for Economic Co-operation and Development, and later within the context of the EEC and European Free Trade Association. This meant that export-oriented growth strategies could now be, and were in fact, adopted throughout Western Europe, while the rapid growth of the period implied that protection was not needed in order to create jobs. There is no doubt that Ireland was slower to jump on the liberalization bandwagon than many other countries, and that this was a costly mistake.

However, the traditional picture of an Ireland that was completely resistant to change before 1958 is overly simplistic. Ireland was a founder member of the OEEC and European Payments Union, the two organizations at the forefront of European trade liberalization during the early 1950s. When it came to quantitative barriers to trade such as quotas, which are more damaging than tariffs, Ireland was the second least protectionist economy in the OEEC in 1950, behind only Switzerland.[23] It subsequently liberalized less rapidly than did other countries, but this was partly because it had less quota-related liberalization to do in the first place. Overall, Ireland emerges

22 The correlation between business cycles in the two countries from 1950 to 1972 inclusive is 0.74, where the business cycle series are simply calculated as deviations from log trend.   23 B. Eichengreen, 'Institutions and economic growth: Europe after World War II' in N. Crafts & G. Toniolo (eds), *Economic growth in Europe since 1945* (Cambridge,

4.8 Was Ireland unusually protectionist? Average tariffs, 1950–72

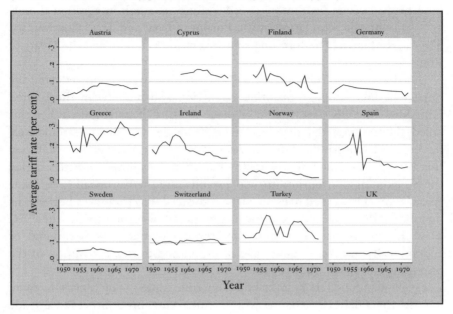

Source: as for figure 4.4.

as an entirely average European country on this dimension of trade policy. It was, however, slower to lower its tariff barriers than core European economies. It behaved, rather, like other peripheral European economies, such as Finland, Greece or Spain, and this relatively slow reduction in tariffs persisted into the 1960s, *after* the famous 1958 move towards greater openness (figure 4.8).

On the other hand, Ireland was relatively precocious in seeking to attract foreign direct investment. The Industrial Development Authority was established as early as 1949, and soon started trying to attract inward multinational investment. The Irish Export Board, soon rechristened Córas Tráchtala, was established in 1950. Tax relief on export profits was introduced in 1956.[24]

Ireland was therefore not as uniquely protectionist and inward-looking during the 1950s as is sometimes claimed. Neither was the timing of its

1996), pp 38–72 at p. 59.   **24** In light of recent controversies it is interesting to note that this soon appeared as a potential concern on the radar screens of foreign governments, appearing to be potentially in breach of the OEEC ban on artificial aids to exporters. The OEEC approved the initiative however, since it seemed to signal a growing outward orientation on the part of the Irish government (Barry and O'Mahony, 2016). F. Barry &

liberalization particularly unusual. It is true that the original six members of
the EEC had begun their move towards greater economic integration as early
as 1951, with the foundation of the European Coal and Steel Community.
They agreed in 1955 to draw up plans for a customs union, and the Treaty of
Rome was signed in 1957.

But the timing of liberalization elsewhere to a large extent reflected the
impact of this initiative on other countries, and notably on the United
Kingdom. The UK first tried to sabotage the EEC negotiations. When this
failed, they attempted to negotiate an OEEC-wide industrial free-trade area,
but completely misjudged the interests of other European countries. When
this attempt also failed, therefore, the British and six other countries signed
the Stockholm Convention in 1960, establishing the European Free Trade
Association. This aimed to establish an industrial free-trade area between its
member states, and ultimately to negotiate an agreement with the EEC
as well. No Western European country, no matter how peripheral or
economically backward, could avoid responding to this disruption of the
prevailing European trade regime.

Spain abandoned its long-standing autarkic trade policy regime in 1959,
joining the OEEC in that year and embarking on a process of trade
liberalization. In 1960 it abolished quantitative restrictions on 90 per cent of
its imports, tariffs were gradually reduced over the succeeding years, and the
country opened itself up, at least to some extent, to inward foreign
investment.[25] Portugal became a founder member of the EFTA, although it
managed to negotiate a transitional deal allowing it to delay tariff reductions
on sectors representing about half of its imports.[26] Finland started lowering
tariffs from 1957 onwards, and signed a trade agreement with the EFTA in
1961.[27] Greece signed an association agreement with the EEC in 1961. This
granted it a twenty-two-year transitional period leading to eventual full
membership; Greece was allowed to lower its tariffs vis-à-vis the EEC
gradually, but benefited from an immediate reduction of EEC tariffs on
Greek exports.[28]

And so it is no surprise that Ireland also took the plunge, at more or less
exactly the same time, and applied for EEC membership in 1961 along with
Britain. Nor is it surprising that when that bid was vetoed by Charles de

C. O'Mahony, *Costello, Lemass and the politics of the new foreign investment regime of the
1950s* (2016), Mimeo.   **25** L.P. de la Escosura & J.C. Sanz, 'Growth and macroeconomic
performance in Spain, 1939–93' in Crafts & Toniolo (eds), *Economic growth in Europe
since 1945*, pp 355–87.   **26** L.F. Costa, P. Lains & S.M. Miranda, *An economic history of
Portugal, 1143–2010* (Cambridge, 2016), pp 308–9.   **27** T. Paavonen, 'Finland and the
question of West European economic integration, 1947–1961', *Scandinavian Economic
History Review*, 52 (2004), 85–109.   **28** A. Freris, *The Greek economy in the twentieth*

Gaulle in 1963 – something for which Irish policy makers can hardly be blamed – Ireland unilaterally cut its tariffs. It did so again in the following year, and in 1965 signed the Anglo-Irish Free Trade Agreement (AIFTA). At this stage Ireland was fully committed to eventual EEC membership, which was finally achieved in 1973.

What *was* unusual about Irish trade liberalization was the extent to which it remained focused on the economic relationship with Britain. To be sure, AIFTA was seen as a stepping stone towards eventual EEC membership, but despite this European motivation, the reality was that Ireland was not yet well integrated with the European economy as a whole. And this was a problem, since access to the British market alone was a far less appealing carrot to dangle in front of potential multinational investors than access to the much larger and more dynamic EEC market.

This leads us to the third explanation for Ireland's relatively poor performance during Europe's golden age. If the poor performance in the 1950s was due to protectionism, and if, as the conventional wisdom has it, Ireland liberalized in a rush from 1958 onwards, then why was its performance so disappointing between 1960 and 1973? The comparison with other peripheral European economies, in particular Greece and Portugal, is illuminating. As we have seen in figure 4.7, Greece and Portugal grew extremely rapidly during this period, while Ireland remained an underperformer. And as we have also seen, in figure 4.8, Greek tariffs were even higher than Irish ones during the 1960s. What can explain the superior performances of Greece and Portugal? Why did Ireland not keep pace?

A key factor in the Greek success story was the country's association agreement with the EEC. Foreign direct investment had been encouraged since the early 1950s, when a series of FDI-friendly policies were introduced,[29] but tariff-free access to EEC markets provided an essential additional stimulus to inward investment. Between 1962 and 1964, more than three-fifths of all manufacturing investment was foreign, according to Kopsidis and Ivanov, who argue that FDI during this period 'diversified and modernized Greek industry'.[30] Continent-wide markets for cheap consumer goods produced in Greece also benefited traditional Greek light industry.

In Portugal too, EFTA membership is seen as having been crucial in promoting a more outward-looking and dynamic economy. According to one estimate, annual inflows of foreign direct investment were more than thirty

century (London, 1986), pp 201–2.   **29** Freris, *The Greek economy in the twentieth century*, pp 171–2.   **30** M. Kopsidis & M. Ivanov, 'Industrialization and de-industrialization in southeast Europe, 1870–2010' in K.H. O'Rourke & J.G. Williamson (eds), *The spread of modern industry to the periphery since 1871* (Oxford, 2017), pp 91–114 at p. 108.

4.9 Initial income and subsequent growth, 1954–73

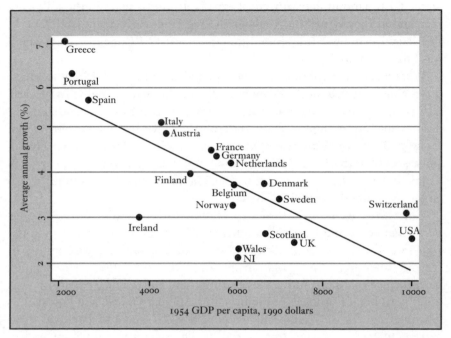

Source: as for figure 4.3. Wales and Northern Ireland: data underlying Dorsett (2013), cited in note 35, graciously provided by author. Scotland: data graciously provided by Brian Ashcroft.

times higher during the 1960s than they had been between 1943 and 1960.[31] Portuguese accession to the EEC in the 1980s would lead to a further step increase in inward foreign investment, as happened also in Spain.[32]

A key difference, therefore, between the Irish case, on the one hand, and the Portuguese and Greek cases on the other, was that Ireland had neither an association agreement with the EEC, nor membership of the EFTA.[33] We tend to assume that once Ireland had signed the AIFTA, it was to all intents and purposes a free trader, and there is something to this. Local firms had to adjust to British competition, and this was good for efficiency. But there is a

31 According to Ferreira da Silva, the inflow in 1961 was as high as the total inflow experienced during the entire 1950s. Das Neves (1996), on the other hand, downplays the role of FDI during the 1960s. A.I. Ferreira da Silva, 'Multinationals and foreign direct investment: the Portuguese experience (1900–2010)', *Journal of Evolutionary Studies in Business*, 2 (2016), 40–68.   32 F. Barry & J. Bradley, 'FDI and trade: the Irish host-country experience', *Economic Journal*, 107 (1997), 1798–1811 at 1809.   33 Recall that EFTA aimed not only to dismantle industrial tariffs between its own member states, but eventually to negotiate tariff reductions vis-à-vis the EEC as well.

4.10 Irish GNP per capita as percentage of UK and French GDP per capita

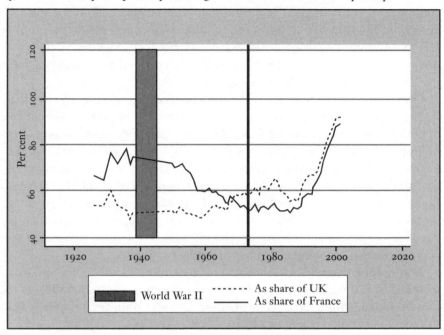

Source: as for figure 4.3. Note: the vertical line denotes 1973.

4.11 Initial income and subsequent growth, 1973–90

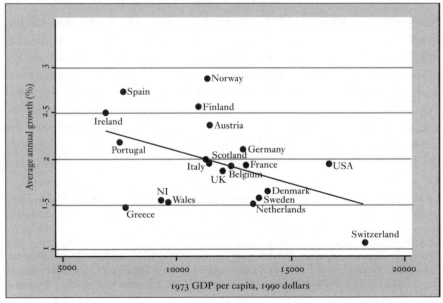

Source: as for figure 4.3.

big difference between accepting free trade between oneself and just one country, and becoming part of a continent-wide customs union. Until EEC accession, the IDA had to try to sell Ireland as an export platform into the UK and Commonwealth, but this was never as effective a sales pitch as the one we were able to make after 1973. From then on, Ireland was selling into the EEC as a whole, and that made all the difference.

One very striking feature of the data between 1954[34] and 1973 is that Ireland's growth performance was very similar to the growth performances of both Northern Ireland and Wales. All three economies seem to have been underperforming in a very similar way, growing less rapidly than they should have been given their initial income levels (see figure 4.9).[35] This suggests that all three economies were facing a common problem or set of problems. Some of these may have been institutional in nature, such as a fragmented trade-union structure, which made the corporatist arrangements then in vogue on the Continent difficult to achieve.[36] But an excessive reliance on the sluggish British economy is another plausible candidate.

In consequence, while GDP per capita grew more rapidly in Ireland than in the UK during the 1960s (see figure 4.10), this was not sufficient to prevent Ireland falling even further behind a major Continental economy like France. This would change in 1973.

IRELAND IN EUROPE

As figure 4.10 shows, Ireland immediately stopped falling further behind France once it entered the EEC in 1973: Campos et al. estimate that membership boosted Ireland's per capita growth rate by almost 2 percentage points.[37] Of course, many other events were shaking up the international economic landscape at this time, most obviously the oil crises of 1973 and 1979. These led to a decade or more of high unemployment, high inflation, and even higher unemployment as governments attempted to lower the inflation rate. All of these developments hurt Ireland. And yet, even before the Irish economic miracle of the 1990s, Ireland was once again growing just

34 Which is when reliable GDP estimates for Wales and Northern Ireland become available.   35 R. Dorsett, 'The effect of the Troubles on GDP in Northern Ireland', *European Journal of Political Economy*, 29 (2013), 119–33.   36 C. Ó Gráda & K. O'Rourke, 'Irish economic growth, 1945–88' in Crafts & Toniolo (eds), *Economic growth in Europe since 1945*, pp 388–426.   37 N.F. Campos, F. Coricelli & L. Moretti, 'Economic growth and political integration: estimating the benefits from membership in the European Union using the synthetic counterfactuals method', *Centre for Economic Policy Research Discussion Paper 9968* (2014).

4.12 Initial income and subsequent growth, 1990–2001

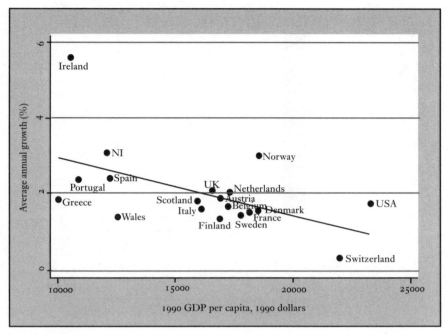

Source: as for figure 4.3.

about as rapidly as would have been predicted within a convergence framework (see figure 4.11). Foreign direct investment, based on selling into the EEC, was the major factor improving Irish performance from 1973 onwards, although the Common Agricultural Policy clearly also helped. We would certainly have done even better had it not been for the budgetary mistakes of the late 1970s, and their inevitable consequences in the succeeding decade.

The second major turning point in Ireland's economic fortunes was, of course, the short period between 1987 and 1990. During the 1990s, Ireland was, as we all know, an extraordinary over performer (see figure 4.12). A comparison between Ireland, on the one hand, and Northern Ireland, Scotland and Wales on the other, is informative (see figure 4.13). Ireland had been gaining ground on these UK regions from 1960 onwards, as we have already seen, which might represent a gradual process of convergence occurring within the British and Irish regional economy. The acceleration from 1990 onwards, however, represents something entirely different. It seems clear, not only that the European Union was fundamental in transforming the Irish economy, but that Irish independence was essential in

4.13 Incomes relative to UK, 1924–2001

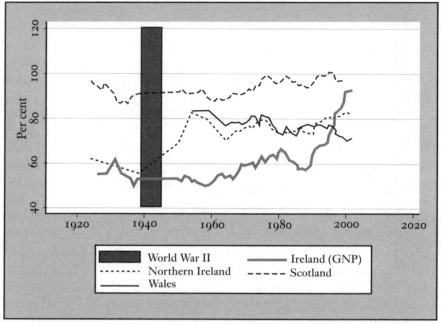

Source: as for figure 4.9.

exploiting the opportunities which the European Union afforded. As the figure suggests, we would never have done anywhere near as well as we in fact did, had we remained a mere region of the United Kingdom.

Policy flexibility at a time of rapid change was essential, and that is what independence gave us. It's important to note that Ireland is not the only small European country to have performed well in the context of a globalizing economy. There is a well-established political science literature that shows how other small European countries, in Scandinavia and elsewhere, have been able to respond nimbly and flexibly to changing international market conditions, in ways that larger countries have found more difficult.[38] But EU membership, and the single-market programme of the late 1980s and early 1990s, were essential in allowing Ireland to finally reap the full economic rewards of its independence.

The policy mix that we adopted is well known: a low corporation tax and other incentives for inward investment, including investment in education and infrastructure. Cormac Ó Gráda and I have also argued that social

38 P.J. Katzenstein, *Small states in world markets: industrial policy in Europe* (Ithaca, NY, 1985).

4.14 OECD and peripheral European GDP volatility, 1960–2014

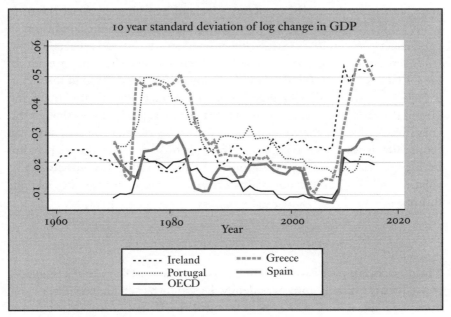

Source: as for figure 4.3.

partnership was important, moderating wage growth and providing a stable industrial-relations environment.[39] Underpinning everything were two crucial factors: our political independence, which allowed us to adopt a policy mix well suited to our own circumstances; and our membership of the European single market, without which none of this would have worked. Political independence and EU membership were never fundamentally at odds with each other in Ireland; each was required to give full effect to the other. Our independence would not have worked as well as it did without the EU; our EU membership would not have worked as well as it did without independence.

Since 1973, and even more so since 1990, Ireland has become a hyper-globalized country whose subsequent economic history has mirrored the ebbs and flows of the global economy, in highly exaggerated fashion. The recession of the early 1980s, as inflation was squeezed out of the Western economic system; the Clinton/Greenspan IT boom of the 1990s; the credit

[39] Just as it had done on the Continent during the European golden age (Eichengreen, 1996). C. ÓGráda & K.H. O'Rourke, 'Living standards and growth' in J. O'Hagan (ed.), *The economy of Ireland: policy and performance of a European region* (Dublin, 2000), pp 178–204.

and housing bubbles of the Great Moderation; the economic collapse of 2008, and the subsequent recovery – Ireland experienced all of them, in spades. This heightened sensitivity to international economic conditions in part reflects the country's extraordinary openness, but it also reflects an Irish tendency to spend when times are good, and to borrow when they are not. In the OECD as a whole, GDP volatility declined after the turmoil of the 1970s; in Ireland, if anything it increased – even before the extraordinary bubble and bust of the early twenty-first century (see figure 4.14). It seems as though this volatility is to some extent a common feature of the peripheral European economies I have been comparing Ireland to throughout this paper; but noting this does nothing to diminish the problem, and moderating this volatility needs to be a major policy priority for the country going into the future.

THE CHALLENGES OF BREXIT

The other major priority is adjusting to Brexit, and, perhaps, to the economic consequences of a Trump presidency. Exactly what challenges Brexit will imply is unclear, and will remain so until the British government finally decides what it wants. There is no doubt but that a hard Brexit would be damaging to Ireland. It would be an unfriendly act, not in the sense that the British would be trying to hurt Ireland – of course they would not be – but in the sense that the damage a hard Brexit would cause us would be of no great concern to them either way. It was ever thus: England is a big country, and can't reasonably be expected to do anything other than to pursue its own best interest as it sees it, without taking too much account of the interests of the smaller countries on these islands. That is why in my view Irish independence was always both inevitable and desirable, but that is another matter.

Because a hard Brexit would damage Irish interests, it is logical that we should desire that our nearest neighbours not proceed with it. But it is important that this desire not lead us to engage in wishful thinking. Once Britain has left the EU, the EU will be obliged under World Trade Organization rules to impose tariffs on imports coming from the UK. This is not something that the EU can avoid: if it were not to do this, it would be discriminating against its other trading partners, and that is illegal. The only circumstance in which the EU would be allowed to not impose tariffs on British goods is if there were a legally registered free-trade agreement of one sort or another in place at the moment that Brexit occurs. And there are two major problems here. First, it is far from clear that it will be legally possible to negotiate a free-trade agreement with the UK while it remains a member

4.15 The destination of Irish exports, 2015

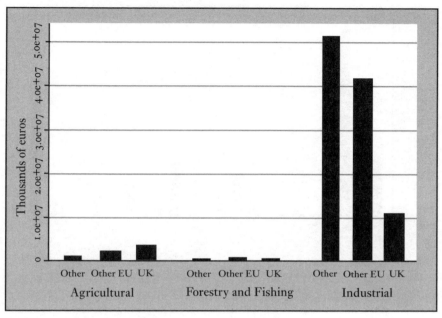

Source: Central Statistics Office.

of the EU. But even if it is legally possible, which seems doubtful, there is a second, practical consideration, which is that it takes years for trade deals to be negotiated and ratified. The chance of a comprehensive deal between the EU and UK being ironed out within two years is zero.

So if we are to avoid tariff barriers, either between the Republic of Ireland and the North, or, preferably, between Ireland and Britain, we are going to need a transitional arrangement of some sort that can be easily agreed within the two-year framework, without too much substantive negotiating being involved. A detailed bespoke transitional agreement seems impossible – it will be just as difficult to negotiate as a permanent agreement, in part because transitional agreements often last a very long time. And so it will have to be an off-the-shelf arrangement – temporary membership of the European Economic Area for example, or temporary membership of the EU customs union. If the British decide that they don't want either of these options, or some other easily available alternative, on even a transitional basis, then hard Brexit will become inevitable. And it is important to be clear that it will be British choices, and not anyone else's, that will have caused this outcome.

The problem for Ireland is that, although our prosperity is based on our membership of the EU single market, a comparatively high share of Irish

4.16 Merchandise trade, goods forwarded (absolute tonnage)

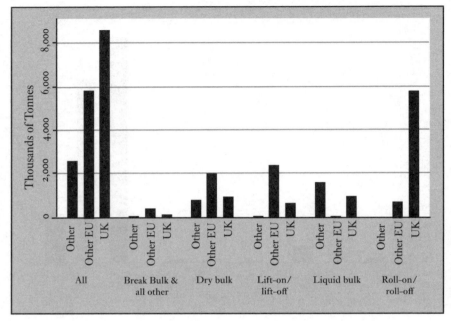

Source: Central Statistics Office.

exports still goes to Britain. It's important to be clear: other European markets are far more important to us than the UK (see figure 4.15). They are, as I have emphasized, the basis of our prosperity. No sane Irish politician would choose the British market over the far larger European one. But Britain is still our major agricultural market, and many of our smaller, more labour-intensive indigenous industries still sell a lot there. This matters, since food and agricultural tariffs are particularly high, and since these sectors are more employment-intensive than some of the higher-profile multinational sectors.

Another potential concern is the very high share of Irish merchandise exports being shipped to, and in some cases through, the United Kingdom (see figure 4.16). Especially worrying is the large share of roll-on roll-off traffic going to the UK; it seems likely that those smaller, labour-intensive firms exporting food and other products, who risk losing sales to the UK, are predominantly exporting their products in this fashion. To what extent might customs delays at Dover and Calais impose extra costs on them when they export to the Continent? We don't know yet, but it seems to me that this is also a potential concern.

What is clear is that Brexit is going to require that we adjust. How well we adjust will define our future prosperity over the course of the next couple of decades. But we're going to have to adjust anyway, probably, since the kind of hyper-globalization that we have been so good at exploiting is becoming politically unsustainable throughout the Western world. We don't want to find ourselves on the wrong side of history.

We are hardly the first country to have faced this sort of external trade shock. Finland's problems in 1991, when it found itself having to cope with the consequences of the breakup of the Soviet Union, with whom a huge share of its trade had previously been conducted, were probably more serious than those that we are likely to face; its adjustment was exemplary. Late nineteenth-century Denmark found itself facing higher tariff barriers in its traditional German market after 1879, as well as prohibitions on live cattle exports that lasted several years. It also successfully adjusted, switching into dairying and other activities targeting the British, rather than the German, market. Ireland itself had to adjust during the 1960s, as the manufacturing industries that had been built up during the protectionist era became exposed to international competition. We will have to do so again.

It is time to conclude. I have argued that Irish prosperity in recent decades has depended both on our membership of the European Union, and on our political independence, which allowed us to make the most of that membership, by giving us the freedom to make policy choices that were suited to our own circumstances. Much the same has been true for several other small European countries: once again, our own national story is part of a larger picture. We are not so different as we sometimes think we are.

Of course we have made mistakes – it would have been odd had we not done so, especially in the context of the twentieth century. But our mistakes were not particularly unusual, or especially egregious; and they were eventually remedied. And isn't it the case, whether we are dealing with individual human beings, or with entire nations, that having the freedom to make your own mistakes, and learn from them, rather than being permanently subjected to the consequences of other peoples' mistakes, is what freedom is all about?

The role of education in addressing the challenges of the twenty-first century

Louise Richardson

In thinking about my talk today I realized immediately that my title was way too ambitious. There are a great many challenges of the twenty-first century and most of them are likely to be revealed as the century progresses. My expertise, moreover, is limited to university education and that will be my focus today. A more accurate title therefore might have been: 'The role of universities in addressing some of the challenges evident at the beginning of the twenty-first century'. In speaking on this subject, I will be relying on the work of some of my Oxford colleagues, especially Diego Gambetta and Senia Pašeta.

CHALLENGES 1916, 2016, 2116

What are these challenges? My list is by no means exhaustive but I would suggest: political violence, inequality, climate change, globalization and technological change, and I will focus on the first two. It is perhaps worth noting that each one of these challenges transcends national borders. From the vantage point of 1916, these challenges looked very different. The priority then was political violence, as Europe was subsumed in an orgy of mass slaughter as the powers fought for dominance. From the vantage point of 2116, I expect the priority will be climate change. I predict that our successors will look back on us today and wonder how we could have sat on our hands while evidence of the calamitous consequences of climate change mounted monthly.

In 1916 the political leaders in London were preoccupied by political violence, engaged as they were in the war to end all wars. Two years after the start of the war and months before the slaughter at the Somme, the allies had already lost several hundred thousand men. The savage costs of the war greatly exceeded all their expectations. They perceived the Easter Rising as a treacherous stab in the back of a nation fighting for its very survival against the German army. They had more pressing demands upon their attention than the social inequality rampant across Britain. The leaders of the Rising in Dublin were interested in establishing rather than transcending national borders. They had a very different perspective on political violence. Perceiving Britain's difficulty as Ireland's opportunity, they saw their attempt at political violence as a noble means of securing Irish freedom, succeeding where six previous attempts had failed.

Some, followers of James Connolly, were motivated by a desire to address social inequality in Dublin, but for most the commitment to equality was more abstract. The 1916 declaration of independence spoke of 'cherishing all the children of the nation equally' of 'equal rights and equal opportunities to all citizens' and of 'suffrages of all her men and women'. The priority, however, was physical force to achieve Irish freedom: 'the right of the people of Ireland to the ownership of Ireland, and to the unfettered control of Irish destinies, to be sovereign and indefeasible'. They sought equality for the Irish nation among the recognized governments of the world rather than social equality for the Irish population. Like most revolutionaries, they were vague on what precisely this freedom would entail.

I expect that the vast majority of the population of both Britain and Ireland were primarily concerned, then as now, with their own and their families' security and well-being.

While late-nineteenth-century advances in transportation and tele-communications had increased trade and cultural diffusion among, especially, Western nations, the term 'globalization' was unknown in 1916 and the phenomenon was certainly not considered a threat or even a challenge. Indeed, many in Britain, influenced by Norman Angell's *The grand illusion*, naively thought increased trade across Europe made a world war impossible.[1] In fact, Angell's argument was that economic interdependence made war futile, a more plausible claim.

In 2016 we are witnessing a popular revolt against globalization. Electorates across Europe and America, mobilized by populist – and often unscrupulous – politicians, are voting against the proponents of globalization, insisting that they are losing their jobs and their livelihoods as a result, either, because of outsourcing to countries with lower labour costs, or, to the importation of immigrants willing to accept lower wages. Support for Brexit in the United Kingdom and for Trump in the US are only two of the most visible exemplars of this trend. It is impossible to foresee the vantage point of 2116, but it is hard to imagine that the clock can be turned back on globalization. We can only hope that governments will make more concerted efforts to ensure that the benefits of globalization are more broadly distributed.

1 N. Angell, *The grand illusion* (New York, 1910).

Technological change is a constant. Warfare has long served as a catalyst for technological innovation. The 1914–18 war witnessed a transformation in weaponry with the introduction of tanks, machine guns, poison gas, submarines, flamethrowers and even air reconnaissance. The transport of troops by railway also transformed the conduct of war. The vast scale of the casualties – estimated at an unimaginable 38 million – was in part due to the introduction of these military innovations and delays in adapting defensive tactics. The pace of technological change has accelerated as the century has progressed and we can be confident that it will continue to do so into the future, to the point where it is hard to imagine how a gathering such as this conference might be conducted, and how we might all travel to it, in 2116.

Having briefly sketched the five challenges I will address, let me now turn to the question of education, and universities in particular. At a time when only a tiny percentage of the population was university-educated, three of the seven signatories on the 1916 declaration of independence were educators: Patrick Pearse, Joseph Mary Plunkett and Thomas MacDonagh. All three were teachers in the school founded by Pearse and MacDonagh, St Enda's. Two other teachers in the school, William Pearse and Con Colbert, were also among those executed in the wake of the Rising.

Pearse cared passionately about education and founded St Enda's in 1908. The school was bilingual, with an unashamedly Celtic and nationalist ethos, teaching valour and heroism refracted through a fascination with mythology. But Pearse was also influenced by the philosophy of Maria Montessori and sought to create a child centred environment focused on personal development, creativity, imagination and intellectual freedom. Drawing on the ancient Celtic tradition of fostering, he saw the role of teachers as fostering the personal development of each individual child. These were radical ideas at the time. In his 1915 polemic, *The murder machine*, he railed against the Irish teaching system which, he argued, perceived and practiced education as a 'manufacturing process'. He wrote:

> Our common parlance has become impressed with the conception of education as some sort of manufacturing process. Our children are the 'raw material'; we desiderate for their education 'modern methods' which must be efficient but cheap; we send them to Clongowes to be 'finished'; when finished they are 'turned out'; specialists 'grind' them for the English civil service and the so-called liberal professions.[2]

2 P.H. Pearse, *The murder machine* (Dublin, 1916), p. 12.

Ever the visionary, he sought to replace this system with one inspired by ancient Celtic traditions, literature and heroic legends that would develop a generation of gallant Gaelic-speaking individuals to fight for the new Ireland. Few proponents of political violence have been as vocal on the subject of education as Pearse. Most are more focused on the evils of the adversary and the tactics required to prevail against them. It is nevertheless difficult to escape the comparison with latter-day conservative madrasas. The educational philosophy of St Enda's, with its focus on the individual development of the child, could hardly be more different from the harsh discipline and rote learning of some madrasas, producing graduates unschooled in any of the skills required for success in the modern world. Where St Enda's attracted the children of the Dublin middle and professional classes, some madrasas attract the children of families who can ill afford to feed much less educate them. Nevertheless, the idea of inculcating the next generation in the ideology of those wishing to overthrow the state and revert to an earlier mythical and halcyon past, is a shared feature.

POLITICAL VIOLENCE

What then of the relationship between education, or universities, and political violence? I think it fair to assume that political violence will remain a challenge for the twenty-first century. As an educator, and one who has spent my career trying to understand the motives of those who resort to terrorism, it is very tempting to see education, and universities in particular, as the antidote to terrorism. If only it were that simple. By terrorism here I mean, simply, the deliberate targeting of non-combatants for a political purpose by a sub-state group.

When I had time to study terrorists I discovered that one attribute they invariably shared was a highly over-simplified view of the world. They tend to see the world in Manichean terms, black and white, good and evil. It goes without saying that they see themselves as good and their opponents as evil. I find it difficult to identify this world view with an education that teaches you to think critically, to question arguments and assumptions, and to look always for the grey. I see the role of education as being, in part, to rob students of their certitudes, and certitude is a requirement of those willing to sacrifice their lives, and commit atrocities that violate every religious and ethical code known, in pursuit of a goal they are unlikely to achieve.

University education is, in many ways, antithetical to military training. Where universities train students to question, military training teaches obedience. Where universities require consideration, the military requires action. Most importantly, where universities, and especially the humanities, endeavour to inculcate empathy; military action, whether by conventional armies, guerrilla insurgents or terrorists, requires the dehumanizing of the adversary as a prerequisite for killing them.

The British government in 2015 passed into law the Counter-Terrorism and Security Act, which introduced a new statutory duty for universities to have 'due regard to the need to prevent individuals from being drawn into terrorism'. This means that universities are now obliged to engage with what is called the 'Prevent' agenda. The two aspects of this legislation that are of most concern to universities are the obligation to report to the authorities those seen as vulnerable to radicalization, and the infringement of freedom of speech entailed in the prohibition on the expression of extremist – including non-violent – speech.

The legislation arose from an understandable concern about the radicalization of young people. While not ostensibly focused on any particular group, there is no doubt in anyone's mind that the target, in fact, is Islamic extremism. Universities have two concerns. If Muslim students fear being reported to the authorities, they are less likely to avail themselves of the support facilities available at university. Moreover, they are more likely to feel suspect and unwelcome, and hence less likely to integrate into university life. An even bigger concern is the threat to the freedom of expression that is the hallmark of any university worth the name. An amendment to the legislation attached in the house of lords allowed universities to have particular regard to their obligation to defend free speech, which provides some protection against the more draconian aspects of the original bill. Nevertheless, with annual reporting to the Higher Education Funding Council for England (HEFCE) on the measures being taken to ensure that 'extremist speech' is not expressed at universities, there is necessarily a chilling effect on free speech.

My own view is that universities should welcome the expression of all legal speech on campus. It is precisely at universities where such speech can be openly challenged. As teachers I believe we have an obligation to model to our students how to respond to speech they find objectionable. We should do so in a spirit of what my colleague, Timothy Garton Ash, calls 'robust civility'. Extremist speech is vaguely defined in legislation as speech expressing vocal or active opposition to British values. I would think that British values are sufficiently robust to withstand such criticism and indeed that it is a core British value to respect the right to criticize the powers that be.

It is true, of course, that some terrorists have been radicalized while at university; given the demographic of the university population it would be astonishing if they were not. The Centre for Social Cohesion claims that 30 per cent of individuals involved in Islamist-inspired terrorist attacks in the UK had attended British universities or third-level colleges. The iron law of social science, of course, is that correlation does not imply causation. It does not follow that they were radicalized at university. We have no way of knowing how many young people went to university with radical views that were changed by their education.

Cases that are cited are King's College London graduates Asif Hanif and Omar Khan Sharif, who carried out a suicide bomb attack in Tel Aviv in 2003, and Abdullah Ahmad Ali, who participated in the plot to carry out a liquid bomb attack on trans-Atlantic flights in 2007. He had attended London City University. Another example was Kafeel Ahmad, a member of the Islamic Society at Queen's University, Belfast, who died trying to detonate an explosive outside Glasgow airport. I've seen no evidence to suggest that they were radicalized at university. By and large, young men carry out terrorist attacks. There are lots of young men at university. Prisons, which also hold large numbers of young men, are infinitely more effective breeding grounds for terrorists.

One case in which a terrorist claimed to have been radicalized at university is Umar Farouk Abdulmutallab, variously known as the Underpants Bomber or the Christmas Bomber, who is said to have been radicalized at University College London, where he was president of the Islamic Society. His parents were belatedly aware of his radicalization and went to considerable lengths to arrest it. He studied in Yemen both before and after his time in UCL, so it is reasonable to assume some of the radicalization may have taken place there. He was sentenced to life in prison for trying to blow up a Detroit-bound plane on Christmas Day 2009.

Another well-known case is that of Omar Sheikh who was convicted of the brutal murder of Daniel Pearl. He wrote in his confession that while a student at the London School of Economics in 1992, 'Bosnia Week' was observed and a number of documentary films were shown. He wrote that one film in particular, *The death of a nation*, which depicted Bosnian Muslims being murdered by Serbs, 'shook my heart' and launched his political awakening and subsequent radicalization. He helped to organize a student conference on Bosnia and then began fundraising for a convoy of materials for Bosnia. Soon he was making contact with Islamic militants. It is hard for me to see how the LSE can be held accountable for his radicalization. We don't know how many other students participated in the same activities, watched the same films, even contributed to relief materials, without being radicalized.

While I would insist that universities cannot be blamed for the radicalization of their students, it is the case that many terrorists are, in fact, highly educated. In terrorist organizations, as in most others, the leaders tend to be different from the followers. They often, for example, come from higher educational and socio-economic backgrounds. The leader not only arranges training but provides an ideology, identifies the enemy, articulates a strategy. In some cases the leader becomes the personification of the group or ideology. Some leaders have almost god-like status among their followers, such as Osama Bin Laden of Al-Qaeda, Vellupillai Prabakharan of the Sri Lankan Tamil Tigers, and Shoko Asahara of the Japanese group Aum Shinrikyo (known among other things for the unusually high educational attainment of its members). Some organizations create a cult of personality around their leaders, such as Abimael Guzmán of the Peruvian Shining Path and Abdullah Öcalan of the Turkish PKK.

Leaders of terrorist movements tend to be older and more highly educated than their followers no matter what part of the world they come from. In Latin America, while the long-time leader of the FARC, Manuel Marulanda Velez, was not thought to have been highly educated, Brazil's Carol Marighella was a civil-engineering dropout. Raul Sendic, leader of the Uruguayan Tupamaros, was a lawyer. Mario Roberto Santucho, leader of the Argentine ERP, was an economist and Guzmán a professor of anthropology. In Europe most of the leaders of the Italian Red Brigades were university professors. Many of the members of the Baader-Meinhof Gang in Germany were university dropouts. Abdullah Öcalan of the PKK studied law and political science.

Islamist groups appear to recruit successfully from all sections of society. Famously, Osama Bin Laden was a multimillionaire and studied economics. His second in command, Ayman al-Zawahiri, is a doctor, as was George Habash, the leader of the Popular Front for the Liberation of Palestine, and Abdul Aziz Rantisi, one of the founders of Hamas. Mohammad Atta, the leader of the 9/11 team, earned a PhD in urban planning. Sheikh Ahmed Yassin, the spiritual leader of Hamas, trained as a teacher, and Yasser Arafat as an engineer.

Marc Sageman studied the biographies of 171 members of Al-Qaeda and found that two-thirds were middle or upper class and that 60 per cent had attended university, while several had doctorates.[3] Similarly, Gilles Keppel

---

3 M. Sageman, *Understanding terror networks* (Philadelphia, 2004).

studied 300 Islamic militants in Egypt and found that they too were more highly educated and of higher social-economic status than most terrorists.[4] Peter Bergen and Swati Pandey's examination of the backgrounds of seventy-five terrorists responsible for some of the most damaging attacks found that 53 per cent had attended college or had doctorates from Western universities, while two others were working on PhDs.[5] While every terrorist group needs foot soldiers as cannon fodder, Islamist groups have successfully recruited a cadre of highly educated followers. Men such as Omar Sheikh and Mohamad Atta are required for the kind of international operations that necessitate international travel and operating in different societies. Moreover, increased reliance on the internet for secure transnational communication requires operatives with some technological facility.

Universities then do not cause radicalization but nor has university education prevented individuals from becoming terrorists. Recent empirical work by Diego Gambetta and Steffen Hertog has shed a fascinating new light on the more nuanced relationship between university education, and in particular, courses of study, and terrorism.[6] Ever since Ted Gurr's seminal book *Why men rebel* was published in 1970, we have known about the power of relative deprivation.[7] This is the view that it is not one's objective condition but rather one's relative condition that incites rebellion. The Peruvian Shining Path would be a case in point. The government introduced universities in the remote regions like Ayacuchu to bring higher education to the indigenous population. They received the education and emerged with heightened expectations into an economy that could not employ them. They were easily radicalized by Abimael Guzmán, offering both a Maoist explanation for their predicament and a means to redress it.

Gambetta and Hertog have focused on contemporary Islamic extremists, and while their findings need to be treated with caution, as the numbers are low and accurate information hard to attain, they provide empirical support for claims we have long felt intuitively, namely that particular types of terrorist groups tend to recruit people with particular educational backgrounds.[8] They too find some support for the motivating power of a sense of relative deprivation, which they find consistent with the growth and decline of various professions – engineers, doctors, teachers and lawyers – in opposition movements in Islamic countries over the course of a century.

4 G. Keppel, *Muslim extremism in Egypt: the prophet and the pharaoh* (Berkeley, 1995).
5 P. Bergen and S. Pandey, 'The madrassa myth', *New York Times*, 14 June 2005.
6 D. Gambetta and S. Hertog, *Engineers of jihad* (Princeton, 2016). 7 T.R. Gurr, *Why men rebel* (Princeton, 1970). 8 The next several paragraphs rely heavily on the work of Gambetta and Hertog, cited in n. 6.

They found very few graduates in extremist groups in countries with good labour-market opportunities. Medicine and engineering are the two subjects with the highest status and highest entry requirements across the Islamic world. They found that engineers were prominent in Islamic radicalism in the 1970s in countries undergoing economic crises, but not earlier. They also found that there were very few engineers in Islamist movements in Saudi Arabia, where there were very good labour-market opportunities.

They found that the core of the Islamist movement emerged from would-be elites not the poor and dispossessed. They demonstrate that university graduates are over-represented among Islamic radicals, and that the higher the level of education the greater the likelihood of joining a violent group, and that those with the most demanding degrees – like engineering and medicine – have a greater likelihood of joining. They found that across groups and countries, relative to the male population, the number of engineers in extremist groups is fourteen times what you would expect, and four times what you would expect relative to university graduates.

Gambetta and Hertog find that engineers radicalize in the Islamic world partly as a result of acute relative deprivation but that they radicalize disproportionally even in the absence of frustrated aspirations, as shown by their presence among Islamists based in South Asia and the West. In short, engineers prefer to join violent rather than peaceful Islamist opposition groups. Engineers prefer to join religious rather than secular and nationalist groups. Doctors are better represented than engineers among non-violent Islamists; when given the choice, doctors opt for secular groups. Engineers who do join radical groups do so with special intensity and devotion with a particular bias for religious extremism. They are more committed and less likely to defect. In fact, the odds of an engineer defecting are 40 per cent of what one would expect given their numbers.

There are lots of similarities between Islamist groups and violent right-wing groups, and they are very different from left-wing groups. Radical right-wing movements aim for ethnic and cultural purification, Islamists aim for religious purification, and both aim for purity of social mores and share social conservatism. They tend to share a nostalgia for a lost past, a focus on tradition, and an obsession with order, hierarchy and strong identity boundaries. Left-wing groups are very different, and while engineers are frequently found among right-wing extremist movements in the developed world, they rarely join left-wing groups.

One argument would be that recruiters want engineers because of their practical skills, but this is not consistent with the evidence. Groups in which members are selected by recruiters have fewer engineers than groups where they are self-selected, and besides, left-wing groups also need practical engineering skills but rarely get them.

In stark contrast, humanities and social science graduates are strongly represented in left-wing groups but almost entirely absent from right-wing and Islamist ones. Moreover, the odds of a humanities graduate defecting from the group are fourteen times greater than you would expect from their numbers. Relative to engineers the odds of a humanities student defecting is forty times greater. Doctors, on the other hand, defect in proportion to their presence in the group. It is also perhaps worth pointing out that women are relatively rare in Islamist and right-wing groups but quite evident in left-wing groups.

What then is the role of universities in addressing the challenge of political violence in the twenty-first century? As I have attempted to demonstrate, a university degree is no antidote to political violence, but I believe that an education is. As engines of our economies, universities can help to undermine the emergence of the sense of relative deprivation that arises from the frustrated ambitions of the highly educated in economies that cannot absorb them, deploy their skills or enable them to realize their ambitions. But if universities focus exclusively on training a skilled workforce, we lose the opportunity to provide an education that is so much broader and more important. An education that produces a generation accustomed to thinking critically, acting ethically and always questioning – whether it is the doctrines of the government of the day or the ideologies of those who wish to overthrow it – will ensure a generation that will question those proponents of violence. An education that teaches empathy with others, that exposes its students to a cosmopolitan community of scholars, that delights in difference rather than fears it, and that inculcates the belief that truth is an aspiration not a possession, will produce a generation that will reject any effort to impose orthodoxy.

INEQUALITY

As well as engines of the economy, universities have long served as drivers of social mobility. They will need to continue to do so, and to do so with more energy and creativity, if we are to redress societal inequality. The centrality of the issue of inequality in Western democracies was captured by the reception accorded Thomas Piketty's book, *Capital in the twenty-first century*.[9] He focused on wealth inequality in the US and Europe since the

9 T. Piketty, *Capital in the twenty-first century* (Cambridge, MA, 2014).

eighteenth century, and argued that the rate of return on capital is greater than economic growth over the long term, resulting in a concentration of wealth and social and economic instability. The book reached the number one slot on the *New York Times* best-seller list for hardcover non-fiction and became the greatest ever sales success for Harvard University Press. Clearly he was onto something, the same something, indeed, as the Occupy movement.

The question of inequality is too broad for consideration here and the gravest inequality, of course, is between rich and poor countries. My focus is on equality of access to education in countries like ours. By comparison, across Africa only 6 per cent of the population are university-educated and even there the variation among countries is significant.

Compared to the universities of 1916, today's universities are bigger, their students come from more diverse socio-economic backgrounds and are, of course, markedly more female. The transformation of the role of women in Irish universities is captured by the fact that in 1898 women made up 0.8 per cent of medical students matriculating at Irish universities. In 2008 they were 75 per cent.[10]

Queen's College, Belfast was the most progressive of all Irish university colleges and was proud of its record on female education. Queen's admitted women to its honours classes in 1882 (and to medical classes from 1889). Queen's College, Cork admitted its first female medical students in 1890 and Queen's College, Galway in 1892.

When women were first admitted to study in Galway in 1888 the local Catholic bishop, F.J. McCormack, was furious and had a declaration forbidding women to attend the college read aloud in all Catholic churches in his dioceses. Ironically, University College, Dublin, the college that was seen as being at the centre of the drive for Irish educational equality, was the last institution to hold out against admitting women. It was not until the passage of the National University of Ireland bill in 1908 that women began to be integrated as full members of the college, and even then only after the preferred plan of the Catholic clergy – which was the establishment of separate women's colleges – had not been successful.

Curiously, Catholic women made up 9 per cent of the total number of women at Trinity between 1904 and 1924. This is the same as the percentage of Catholic men, and is a significant figure given the extent of clerical

10 I am indebted to Dr Senia Pašeta, fellow and tutor in history, St Hugh's College, Oxford, and author of *Before the revolution: nationalism, social change and Ireland's Catholic elite, 1879–1922* (Oxford, 1999) and *Irish nationalist women, 1900–1918* (Cambridge, 2013) for the historical data in the following several paragraphs.

disapproval. They must have been pretty brave women, as Catholic opinion was firmly anti-Trinity and, at best, neutral on the issue of university education for women.

The pioneers of the women's education movement were mainly middle class, urban and Protestant. Catholic activists only emerged after the first cohort of Catholics had passed through university and could speak for themselves. Until 1879 the only recognized universities in Ireland were Trinity and the Queen's colleges, and neither was acceptable to the Catholic hierarchy, so there was little chance that the women's cause would be taken up.

A big change occurred in 1878 with the establishment of the intermediate education system and in the following year, the Royal University of Ireland. The first was a new system of secondary education open to all students, based exclusively on exam results, and the second just an examining body based on London University and designed for men to get degrees without having had to attend a Protestant institution like Trinity or a non-denominational one like the Queen's colleges. These initiatives took place without women in mind, though women were beneficiaries. This reinforces my view that all one has to do is create a true meritocracy and women will do fine. By 1884, nine women had graduated from the Royal University with a degree, by 1909 there were 70.

Only five women registered at Queen's College, Cork in the first two years after women were allowed admission, but by 1896 there were thirty. A real breakthrough occurred in that year when two women graduated in medicine, thereby shattering the widely held belief that a degree in arts was the pinnacle of women's achievement. While some professors did refuse to teach women, great advances were made. Alice Perry took a first in engineering in Galway in 1906, becoming the first qualified female engineer in the UK, and possibly the world. Remarkably, she was one of five sisters who all graduated from Queen's College, Galway. (Progress, however, was slow. I'm told that in the 1950s in Galway there was only one woman taking honours mathematics, and she was known, not by her given name, but as 'Honours maths'.) Being one of only a few women did have its compensations. Apparently they were in great demand at college dances. One man recollected that women were so scarce that the men were forced to 'ration our dances among the men, half a dance to one man, and half to another' at the college's annual social.

For centuries universities have deprived themselves of the contributions of half the population by their exclusion of women. Who knows what discoveries might have been made, diseases cured, poems and musical scores written, if women had had access to the same education as men? The same applies today to those who, because of the conditions of their birth – whether they are born in an impoverished or war-torn country or into a deprived or dysfunctional family in a wealthy country – are denied the benefits of a good education, with the result that society in turn is denied their potential contributions.

We have to address the societal inequality that means that the children of middle-class parents have a far greater chance of attaining a university education than the children of immigrants or labourers. In the UK the wealthiest children are four times more likely to go to university than those coming from the poorest families, and seven times more likely to go to a top university than the poorest children. The gap even appears to be widening, notwithstanding considerable effort and expense. In the US a child born into a family with an income in the highest quartile has an 85 per cent chance of earning a university degree. A child born into a family with an income in the lowest quartile has an 8 per cent chance. In Dublin, four out of five young people from well-off areas go to university, but in the most disadvantaged areas it is just one out of 7.5. According to the Organisation for Economic Co-operation and Development, in Ireland 20 per cent of people whose parents did not finish secondary school attain a third-level education, compared to 69 per cent of those whose parents have a third-level education. These figures are broadly comparable to England's 22 per cent and 73 per cent, respectively, and less stark than the US's 13 per cent and 61 per cent.[11] While I see this as morally indefensible, it is also practically damaging, as we are denying ourselves access to the talents of so many people.

These are not easy problems to solve. The key to access to a good university education is good early education. Indeed, increasing evidence is becoming available that attendance at preschool significantly improves one's chances of doing well at school later. A recent Oxford study found that children of all social backgrounds in the UK who attended pre-school were twice as likely to attend the sixth form as those who didn't. This is consistent with American studies on the success of the Head Start preschool program.

One of the great tragedies of our wealthy societies is just how many young people (in the UK this cohort is increasingly white working-class males) are falling off the academic ladder very early on. Universities like mine are constantly being criticized for not accepting more poor students, and there is always more we can do, but the real problem is how few younger people from deprived backgrounds have the academic skills to be competitive for entry into the most selective universities.

11 OECD, *Education at a glance* (2016).

Ireland does better than most countries in the proportion of its population achieving third-level education. According to Eurostat, Ireland has the most higher-education graduates per head of population of all twenty-eight countries of the European Union. The economic benefits of a university education are easy to calculate; the intangible benefits are incalculable but even more profound. In the UK, according to the OECD, those with a bachelor's degree earn 49 per cent more than those with a secondary education. In the US the figure is 60 per cent more; in Ireland it is 63 per cent. For those with graduate degrees in the UK their income is 71 per cent higher than those with a secondary education, in the US the figure is 122 per cent more and in Ireland, 90 per cent more.[12] A report on job creation in the recovery from the financial crisis in the US demonstrated that 99 per cent of job growth went to workers with more than a secondary education. (I think that this statistic alone can explain the phenomenon of Donald Trump.) In other words, workers with bachelor's degrees or above have gained 8.4 million jobs, compared to workers with a high school diploma, who gained 80,000.[13]

I believe that the years between now and 2116 will demonstrate a direct correlation between the ability of universities to educate a broader section of society and the degree of social instability experienced by these societies. The last few months have amply demonstrated, most dramatically in the US but certainly in Britain too, the destabilizing power of an economically disenfranchised population.

OTHER CHALLENGES

Universities also have their part to play in addressing the other challenges I mentioned: climate change, globalization and technological change. They will do so by doing what universities do best: dispassionately and creatively conducting research into critical scientific and societal problems and educating the next generation of students in our methods and conclusions. But we must do more. We must become better in promulgating the results of our research and we must win the respect of our societies for the integrity of our findings. That an unscrupulous politician's claim that 'we have had enough of experts' should find resonance is evidence that we have failed to make our case. If our societies are to make the necessary behavioural changes to accommodate climate change, they must be convinced of the reliability of

12 OECD, *Education at a glance* (2016).   13 A. Carnevale, T. Jayasundera & A. Gulish, *American's divided recovery* (Georgetown, DC, 2016).

our findings. If we want populations to dismantle rather than erect national borders we must present incontrovertible evidence of the benefits of globalization. If we want to master new technologies we must educate not only those with the ability to make scientific discoveries and technological innovations, we must educate a generation with the moral sensitivity to think through the ethical implications of these discoveries and innovation for the rest of society.

This is a lot of responsibility to accord universities, but it was John Stuart Mill, a nineteenth-century advocate of reconciliation with Ireland, the advancement of women and freedom of speech, who said that the purpose of a university was 'the laying open to each succeeding generation ... the accumulated treasures of the thoughts of mankind'.

Irish futures in the Isles and Europe: ten predictions

BRENDAN O'LEARY[1]

Some other contributors to this conference had easy assignments, about the past. By contrast, the *future* has become my responsibility, under the provisional heading of 'new paradigms'. And that was before the referendum on EU membership in the UK in June 2016, which will trigger UKEXIT, or the US presidential elections the following November that foretold Trumpistan. No new paradigms will be offered here, however, because I am not a disciple of Thomas Kuhn.[2] Predictions will be offered because to predict and retrodict are reasonable if difficult endeavours for social scientists, but the predictions to follow will be advanced with modesty because no one knows the future. It is difficult if not impossible to assign probabilities to possible worlds, and potentially successful predictions may become self-refuting because once alerted the relevant agents may organize to prevent feasible forecasts.[3] Nevertheless, we all constantly have to think about possible futures, and I won't cheat on my assignment.

BENEATH THE WAVES?

One possible future of the Isles has already been anticipated (see figure 6.1). This map forecasts the erosion of much of the Isles by the next century: notable projected departures beneath the waves include Dublin, Edinburgh, and London, and, I'm sad to say, Galway. Cork and Belfast, however, would survive the predicted inundations, the first being the city of my birth, the second being the dominant city in the county in which I was high-schooled.

---

1 This paper was in the process of revision before the UK elections in June 2017, but completed after.   2 If paradigms mean integrated frameworks of knowledge that succeed one another without commensurable evidence of growth in knowledge then I am an unbeliever; see especially the first edition of T. Kuhn, *The structure of scientific revolutions* (Chicago, 1970 (1962)). Another reason to avoid talk of paradigms is that Margaret Masterman cruelly identified twenty-one different usages in Kuhn's work, though she tried to reduce them to three; M. Masterman, 'The nature of a paradigm' in I. Lakatos & A. Musgrave (eds), *Criticism and the growth of knowledge* (Cambridge, 1970), pp 59–89. 3 For arguments against historicist confidence see K.R. Popper, *The poverty of historicism* (London, 1957).

6.1 A catastrophic vision of the Isles, 2100

Source: Courtesy of Martin Vargic.

This map suggests a catastrophic future unless we collectively avert the possibilities that flow from climate change. The Trump administration, regrettably, is headed by a salesman who has declared that climate change is a Chinese hoax, and has authorized the increased exploitation of coal supposedly to make America great again. I must apologize as a US citizen because that promise or threat, if fulfilled, would make these islands dirtier and hotter than they need be. As an Irish citizen I observe that one of the advantages of dual citizenship is that the calibre of one elected head of state sometimes consoles one for the pain inflicted by another: President Higgins, thank you for inviting me to this centennial conference on the consequences of national sovereignty.

FALSE PROPHESIES AND PROSPECTS

This map of the Isles' future may galvanize thought on how the Irish in Ireland and beyond may assist in inhibiting climate change, but I shall seek to avoid any further 'catastrophism'. I will also avoid discussing the 'mega-trends' affecting Western democratic states: de-democratization, plutocracy, inequality and their spillover effects on parties and mass media; the erosion of historic social-democratic parties; the hollowing out of political parties; xenophobia, Islamism, Islamophobia and revived anti-Semitism; the entrenchment of neo-liberalism – and its discontents; the revival of an assertive/aggressive Russia and the threat that the Trump administration poses to NATO and EU solidarity. All these are important subjects, but we Irish, North and South, cannot be major agents in affecting or reversing these phenomena. Instead I shall consider what Irish political futures, North and South, may look like based on reasonable extrapolations from current conditions. We should do so in full recognition that our futures are not what they used to be in distinct ways that differ from confident estimations made in the 1930s, the 1970s, and at the turn of the second millennium. In the 1930s many British policymakers coded the partition of Ireland as a relative success; that is why they contemplated variations on the same solution for imperial Palestine and India. Yet the negative repercussions of these partitions endure.[4] In the 1970s many accepted Richard Rose's assessment of Northern Ireland, 'The problem is that there is no solution – at least no solution recognizable in those more fortunate parts of the Anglo–American world that are governed with consensus.'[5] Rose was the distinguished author of *Governing without consensus*.[6] Recently, however, people complain that too much consensus is required to make Northern Ireland's new institutions work – we Irish are distinguished by our ingratitude. Lastly, at the turn of the millennium many predicted that the Irish peace process would not succeed. Conor Cruise O'Brien, who had gravitated from left-wing anti-colonialist to right-wing candidate for the United Kingdom Unionist Party, confidently spoke in 1994 of a 'non-existent political solution', and emphatically affirmed of the IRA ceasefire that, 'this is not peace; it is simply a prelude to a different war'. He was not solitary in predicting doom and gloom, or in being a poor forecaster. The Europhobe Michael Gove compared the Good Friday Agreement to the appeasement of Hitler at

4 B. O'Leary, 'Analyzing partition: definition, classification and explanation', *Political Geography*, 26:8 (2007), 886–908.   5 R. Rose, *Northern Ireland: a time of choice* (Basingstoke, 1975), p. 139.   6 R. Rose, *Governing without consensus: an Irish perspective* (London, 1971).

Munich, a cliché, but added a grotesque comparison of his own by suggesting that its content resembled the condoning of paedophilia.[7] In 2004, Gary K. Peatling published *The failure of the Northern Ireland peace process*, and was subsequently joined in his facile pessimism by Geoffrey Wheatcroft's polemic *Yo Blair! Tony Blair's disastrous premiership*.[8]

PEACE AND POWER-SHARING

One does not have to be called Gary, Geoffrey, Michael or Conor to supply erroneous forecasts, and the fate of these pundits' prophecies reminds us of the magnitude of my task. Inspired or disinspired by these examples, let me commence the first of ten predictions. Let us start where we are, contrary to the erroneous expectations of O'Brien, Gove, Peatling and Wheatcroft – that is, in our condition of peace and power-sharing: peace, defined as the absence of war between major armed combatants, and a death toll from political violence of less than twenty-five persons per annum; and intermittently operative power-sharing institutions, including over security and the administration of justice in Northern Ireland, across Ireland, and the Isles. And for now both sovereign jurisdictions on the island are within the EU, the most important power-sharing project in history. Figures 6.2 and 6.3 show that the civilian (non-combatant) death toll flowing from violence over the North has radically diminished, and that total killings have also fallen dramatically – evident in the total annual and cumulative graphs of death tolls in figure 6.3.

These data underpin prediction 1: *Things could always be worse, but peace will continue*. This prediction assumes that neither 'dissident' republican nor loyalist militias have sufficient capacity or support to relaunch a full-scale armed conflict, and that the development of more balanced and impartial policing and judicial institutions has made easier upholding the rule of law and the protection of rights. No assumption has to be made that the Police Service of Northern Ireland (PSNI) or the courts resemble liberal perfection; what matters is whether there is a foreseeable impetus for the various organizations claiming to be the IRA, and the actual residues of the Ulster Defence Association (UDA) and Ulster Volunteer Force (UVF), to build more aggressive campaigns. In my view, there is not. The prospective departure of the UK from the EU is a massively unsettling and deeply

7 M. Gove, *The price of peace: an analysis of British policy in Northern Ireland* (London, 2000).   8 G.K. Peatling, *The failure of the Northern Ireland peace process* (Dublin, 2004); G. Wheatcroft, *Yo Blair! Tony Blair's disastrous premiership* (London, 2007).

6.2 Civilian death toll from the conflict in and over Northern Ireland, 1966–2003

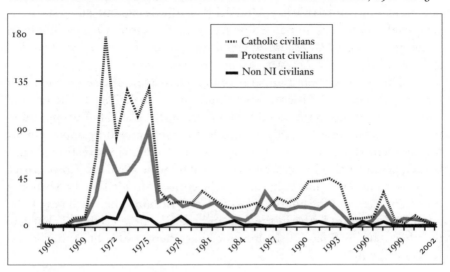

Source: McKittrick, Kelters, et al. (2004).

6.3 Total death toll (cumulative and annual) from political violence in Northern Ireland, 1991–2012

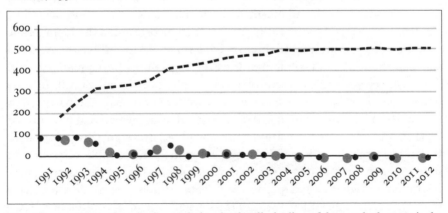

Key: The top line is the actual cumulative death toll; the line of dots at the bottom is the 'smoothed' death toll per annum, which reduces the impact of the Omagh bombing. Source: Police Service of Northern Ireland.

regrettable development, but significant numbers of men and women do not volunteer for war over access to a single market or a customs union; and they usually need credible fears, objectives and prospects of success before they contemplate armed action. So far, with the questionable exception of

Ukraine, no one has yet died over membership of the European Union. This comment does not trivialize UKEXIT in the least, but suggests non-catastrophic outcomes for peace. Prediction 2 follows from what has just been suggested: *UKEXIT, even if it means taking Northern Ireland out of the EU against its will, is unlikely to generate major armed conflict.*

It is, however, sane and imperative to seek to avoid the re-erection of a hard border across the island; wise to minimize the damage to the express and tacit provisions in the Good Friday Agreement related to Europe and in facilitating a borderless island; and prudent to avoid providing opportunities for dissident republicans by erecting customs barriers on a restricted land border, behind which lurk pill boxes manned by armed soldiers. Choices over the future border(s), however, may not be entirely decided by the Irish, the Northern Irish and the political class in Great Britain. There will have to be a border (or more) between the UK and the EU after UKEXIT, but EU member states will have a say in answering where it is to lie, and what its function(s) will be.

THE GOOD FRIDAY AGREEMENT AND ITS DESTABILIZATION

The Good Friday Agreement of 1998 was the major achievement of the last cohort of British, Irish and Northern Irish politicians; it was consolidated by the Saint Andrews Agreement of 2006, which incorporated the Democratic Unionist Party into the settlement.[9] That appeared to resolve the national self-determination question, or at least the procedures for its management. The UK recognized the right of Irish people, North and South, to self-determination, respectively and concurrently, either to maintain partition or to reunify. The Government of Ireland Act of 1920, which had partitioned Ireland and expressed Westminster's absolute sovereignty, was repealed. Ireland as a whole endorsed the 1998 agreement in a double referendum, with 71 per cent and 95 per cent support in the North and South, respectively. Articles 2 and 3 of Ireland's constitution were modified to make reunification possible solely through the separate and joint consent of the two jurisdictions.

The nationalist understanding was that Northern Ireland's status as part of the UK was now a function of Irish choices, not merely the outcome of

9 For discussions, see B. O'Leary, 'The nature of the agreement', *Fordham Journal of International Law*, 24 (1999), 1628–67; J. Ruane & J. Todd (eds), *After the Good Friday Agreement: analyzing political change in Northern Ireland* (Dublin, 1999); J. McGarry & B. O'Leary, 'Introduction: consociational theory and Northern Ireland' in J. McGarry & B. O'Leary, *The Northern Ireland conflict: consociational engagements* (Oxford, 2004).

past British conquest or imposition. In turn, that suggested that Northern Ireland was not now merely a region of the UK granted devolved authority; rather, it was now a 'federacy'.[10] That is to say, it had entrenched, federal-like arrangements that could not be unilaterally altered by Westminster. The new arrangements provided for mutually interconnected institutions – the Northern Ireland assembly and the North–South Ministerial Council – protected by the two sovereign governments in the British–Irish agreement of 1999. Westminster's sovereignty was now qualified: it had to be exercised in accordance with Northern Ireland's new status, respecting its new institutions, including Ireland's role, and respecting Irish self-determination. On this understanding, the entirety of the institutions in the North were not simply revocable acts of delegation by Westminster. This perspective, however, was not shared by unionist lawyers,[11] or by Peter Mandelson when he moved to suspend the new institutions in 2000. The successive suspensions, whatever their justification, strikingly showed that Westminster reserved the same rights as those once contained in Article 75 of the Government of Ireland Act. The attendant controversy was, however, put to one side when the Saint Andrews Agreement was reached; the re-establishment of the Northern Ireland assembly was accompanied by the repeal of the UK's Suspension Act – which had never been formally recognized by Ireland's government.

The inability of the UK to constitutionalize arrangements with its domestic or foreign partners – that is, to establish legally binding institutional arrangements beyond the discretion of a governing majority in Westminster's house of commons – is now being brutally re-advertised. Justice Maguire in Belfast in October 2016,[12] and the UK supreme court, believe that Westminster is not tied by the 1998 agreement and the referendums in both parts of Ireland to a distinct constitution for Northern Ireland that requires legislative consent from the Northern Ireland assembly before the UK begins its secession from the EU. Nor do they believe that the UK government is constrained by how a majority voted in Northern Ireland in the June 2016 referendum. In short, the UK's courts apply the doctrine that whatever the Westminster parliament gives it can take away.

---

10 For discussions of the concept of federacy see D.J. Elazar, *Exploring federalism* (Tuscaloosa, 1987); D.A. Rezvani, 'Shaping the federacy research agenda', *Ethnopolitics*, 6:1 (2007), 129–31; S. Stepan, 'A revised theory of federacy and a case study of civil-war termination in Aceh, Indonesia' in J. McEvoy & B. O'Leary, *Power sharing in deeply divided places* (Philadelphia, 2013), pp 231–52.   **11** A. Morgan, *The Belfast agreement: a practical analysis* (Belfast, 2000).   **12** 18 Oct. 2016 NIQB 85, Maguire J., available at courtsni.gov.uk.

Now, however, the implications of the UK's unconstitutionalized system, with its house of commons controlled before June 2017 by a party with a mandate of 36 per cent of the vote, are even more destabilizing for Northern Ireland's institutions than during the suspension crises of the early part of this century. Intermittent suspension under Labour governments between 2000 and 2006 was at least plausibly driven by efforts to create the conditions for the 1998 agreement to work. Today, however, UKEXIT, as interpreted by the governing Conservatives, has damaged the settled expectations that accompanied the 1998 agreement, namely, joint membership of the European Union by the two sovereign governments, joint commitments to the European Convention on Human Rights and Freedoms, and a borderless Ireland. There is no need to decide whether we are dealing with perfidious or negligently oblivious Albion before issuing prediction 3: *The Westminster government's unilateral decision to modify the terms of the United Kingdom of Great Britain and Northern Ireland's relations with Ireland and the EU will weaken all parties' commitments to the institutions negotiated in 1998/2007.* The first major breach may be a British decision to re-establish direct rule rather than to trigger fresh elections if no executive is formed in the North. Such a decision would require fresh legislation at Westminster, would violate both the Good Friday Agreement and the Saint Andrews Agreement, and would presumably be opposed by any Dublin government. After Ireland's remarkable diplomatic success in placing the stabilization of the Good Friday Agreement in the first basket of issues to be addressed by Michel Barnier's negotiating team in managing the UK's secession from the EU, it would be incoherent for an Irish government to collaborate in the reintroduction of British direct rule in the North.

CONFEDERAL AND FEDERAL FUTURES?

The Good Friday Agreement enabled confederal and federal possibilities. The North-South Ministerial Council, though it has not been the site of major initiatives and activities, could still become the vehicle for a confederal Ireland. The British-Irish Council, more loosely institutionally constructed, and without important obligations, could still become the vehicle to provide unionists with institutional links to the entire Isles in the event of Irish reunification. Unexpectedly, now that Scotland's independence is a feasible political project, rendered thus by the prospect of UKEXIT against Scotland's will, it is possible that the British-Irish Council could become a forum in which post-UKEXIT coordination may be developed among the partner governments, including access to and membership(s) of the single market. It may even become a vehicle through which Scotland might emerge into the EU through confederalizing with sovereign Ireland, but I will not make a speculative prediction in this domain.

The federalizing possibilities latent in the Good Friday Agreement were equally important. Ireland's modified constitution no longer implies that reunification obligates a unitary state – or that negotiators have to follow de Valera's design, which allowed for a subordinate legislature in Belfast.[13] By requiring two referendums, the authorized process of unification would set in place negotiations between two jurisdictions, which conceivably would create a two-unit federation, or inspire some other territorial reconfiguration. But, and it is a big but, after 1998 all such possibilities, confederalizing or federalizing, presupposed a common European roof. The recital to the treaty protecting the Good Friday Agreement referred to the British and Irish governments' wish to 'develop still further the unique relationship between their peoples and the close co-operation between their countries as friendly neighbours and as partners in the European Union'. In 1993 the Downing Street Declaration followed both states' accession to the European Union in the Maastricht Treaty. The North-South Ministerial Council was explicitly mandated to address 'EU issues' (see appendix 1). Jointly these commitments foresaw an internally borderless Europe – though Great Britain and Ireland would continue to operate their own common travel area. The Good Friday Agreement was also peppered with references to the European Convention on Human Rights and Fundamental Freedoms (see appendix 2).

The Good Friday Agreement (GFA) has been a remarkable success even if its full implementation has not occurred, and despite some institutional turbulence. Consociation has worked: the dual premiership and the d'Hondt executive have functioned much better than their critics anticipated.[14] The decade of joint government headed by the DUP and Sinn Féin was, comparatively speaking, an amazing accomplishment. Sinn Féin is now a constitutional republican party, committed to peaceful and democratic

---

13 Article 15.2.2° of Bunreacht na hÉireann allows provision to 'be made by law for the creation or recognition of subordinate legislatures and for the powers and functions of these legislatures'. This clause permitted the recognition of the Northern Ireland parliament within a decentralized unitary state, as a subordinate legislature of the Oireachtas; by contrast, a federal or confederal Ireland could not have been negotiated without constitutional amendments.   14 See J. McEvoy, *Power-sharing executives: governing Bosnia, Macedonia and Northern Ireland* (Philadelphia, 2005); J. McGarry & B. O'Leary, 'Power-sharing executives: consociational and centripetal formulae and the case of Northern Ireland', *Ethnopolitics*, 15:5 (2015), 497–520; C. McCrudden, J. McGarry, B. O'Leary & A. Schwartz, 'Why Northern Ireland's institutions need stability', *Government and Opposition*, 51:1 (2016), 30–58.

politics. Its leaders delivered IRA ceasefires and encouraged the IRA's subsequent internationally monitored disarmament and disbanding; and they have accepted the reformed police and have worked within the GFA's institutions. Even the party's decision not to allow the Northern executive immediately to form after the Spring 2017 elections does not reject the GFA: the party argues that it is asking the DUP to implement agreements already made, rather than asking it to commit to fresh initiatives. The demand that Arlene Foster step aside while enquiries are completed into the 'cash for ash' scandal asks no more than that the DUP leader follow the precedent established when official inquiries took place into Peter Robinson's affairs. On the other side of the divide, the DUP under its founder, and then his successors, has run a power-sharing executive with republicans; participated in all-island and cross-border bodies; and has accepted a significant transformation of the police, as well as the return of justice and policing oversight to the North on a power-sharing basis. No one should be starry-eyed about the two parties' performances, individual or joint, but it would be begrudging not to recognize the transformed scene by comparison with that of the thirty years of major conflict. Nevertheless current appraisals require a downbeat assessment. Prediction 4: *No immediate dismantling of the Strand 1, Strand 2 or Strand 3 institutional outcomes delivered by the Good Friday Agreement is likely, but EU-related matters will have to be renegotiated in ways that are beyond the two sovereign governments' control, and such negotiations may occur in the absence of a functioning Northern executive.*

Between 2007 and the end of 2016 the consolidation of Sinn Féin and the DUP as the respective leaders of their national communities in the North confirmed the 1998 agreement as a 'Nash equilibrium', that is, an equilibrium in which each party responded rationally to its opponents' best moves.[15] Initially both SF and the DUP won increasing vote totals on moderated (not hardening) platforms as champions of their respective voters. The rationale for a deal between the two parties reflected their respective interests. Sinn Féin co-governed the North, and that eased its task of becoming a viable 'coalitionable' and responsible left party in the South.[16]

---

15 For an easy-to-understand account of Nash equilibria see K.G. Binmore, *Fun and games: a text on game theory* (Lexington, MA, 1992). For an account of the post-agreement success of the DUP and SF, see P. Mitchell, G. Evans & B. O'Leary, 'Extremist outbidding in ethnic party systems is not inevitable: tribune parties in Northern Ireland', *Political Studies*, 57:2 (2009), 397–421. 16 John Garry has acutely analyzed Sinn Féin's dual electoral-management strategies in J. Garry, 'Nationalist in the North and socialist in the South? Examining Sinn Féin's support based on both sides of the border' in N. Ó Dochartaigh, K. Hayward & E.M. Meehan (eds), *Dynamics of political change in Ireland: making and breaking a divided island* (London, 2017), pp 145–56.

The DUP claimed that its resistance to the Good Friday Agreement had negotiated the final end of the IRA, and having definitively displaced his rivals in the UUP, Ian Paisley went from being the tribune of Ulster Protestants to the co-governor of the North with the ability to veto republican initiatives. The question ahead is whether this equilibrium is coming to an end.[17] Differently put, do Sinn Féin or the DUP have incentives to disturb the existing equilibrium? The answer is affirmative.

MOVING FROM EQUILIBRIUM OR PICKING AT SCABS?

The DUP increasingly came to use its veto powers in the executive to block all movement on legacy questions from the conflict, and to refuse movement on its prior commitments, making it increasingly difficult for Martin McGuinness and his colleagues to show gains to their base from participation in the Northern executive. While remaining the dominant party of Northern nationalism Sinn Féin had to endure losing votes and seats to its left, that is, to the People Before Profit Alliance, an all-island socialist party, in West Belfast and Derry in the 2016 assembly elections. The UKEXIT referendum, the 'cash for ash' scandal, and McGuinness' terminal illness accelerated Sinn Féin's reappraisal of its strategy. On a ticket of clean government, pro-Europeanism and obliging the DUP to fulfil its previous commitments, McGuinness precipitated fresh assembly elections, and on an increased turnout his party galvanized its base, restored its electoral growth, and on 2 March 2017 came within a whisker of pipping the DUP for the position of the largest Northern party. Sinn Féin can now negotiate from a position of strength. Neither the DUP nor the London government want a fresh set of Northern elections, and the DUP faces both loss of patronage and influence, and full ownership of the likely negative consequences of UKEXIT for the Northern economy. Arguably Sinn Féin can manage the tensions that John Garry has identified – being nationalist in the North and socialist in the South – by risking a period of direct rule during UKEXIT. Its manifesto platform was headed 'Standing Up For Equality, Respect and Integrity'.

The DUP's position is different, and arguably weaker in the long term, despite its very recent successes in the June 2017 Westminster elections,

17 The formal establishment of arrangements for an opposition are not, in my view, fundamental transformations; they took place within the agreed procedures and settings, even though there were good arguments not to have them or to overstate their significance, C. McCrudden, J. McGarry, B. O'Leary & A. Schwartz, 'Why Northern Ireland's institutions need stability', *Government and Opposition*, 51:1 (2016), 30–58.

which have made it a pivotal party in a hung parliament. The party had been shell-shocked that it had nearly lost the right to nominate the first minister; knew that its leader was in trouble, and that it had also twice lost in Northern Ireland-wide referendums, in 1998 and in 2016; and its smarter operators knew that the party did not speak for all unionists' interests or identities. One astute commentator, Brian Feeney of the *Irish News*, has suggested that Arlene Foster may be the last unionist first minister. I will not follow that prediction, nor will I predict which party blinks first in the current negotiations on doing what may be required to restore the Belfast executive. What is nevertheless worth emphasizing is how precarious the DUP's seat-majority was in 2017, though it won 10 out of the 18 seats available. The easiest way to make this point is to look forward. If the recommendations of the UK boundary commission are implemented in 2018, then a reasonable projection inside the new 17 constituencies in Northern Ireland would suggest that the two parties' positions in seats would be almost exactly reversed. That is, Sinn Féin would win 9 seats (+2), whereas the DUP would win 7 (-3).[18] Among those who would lose their seats would be Nigel Dodds, the DUP's parliamentary leader at Westminster, who is bargaining, as I write, with Theresa May over the terms of a confidence-and-supply pact between the Conservatives and the DUP.

NORTHERN TRANSFORMATIONS

Differently put, underpinning recent party manoeuvring in the North are the long-term consequences of demographic transformations. In 1997, following arguments first made in 1990, I predicted that Ulster unionists would lose their electoral dominance.[19] Readers may therefore agree that some of my past predictions have been correct – though even a stopped clock is right twice a day. Between 1969 and 1989 – over local-government, Westminster, European-parliamentary and assembly elections – there was a long-term growth in the Northern nationalist vote, adding together the votes of Sinn Féin, the SDLP and various all-island socialist parties (see figure 6.4).

Albeit at a slower pace, the Northern nationalist vote continued to rise until it reached an apparent plateau around 2007 (see figure 6.5).

18 See http://www.electoralcalculus.co.uk/googleseats2018.html.   19 B. O'Leary, 'Unionists will lose electoral dominance', *Irish Times*, 2 July 1997; B. O'Leary, 'More green, fewer orange', *Fortnight*, 2 (1990), 12–15.

6.4 Vote share of the Northern nationalist bloc in elections, 1969–89

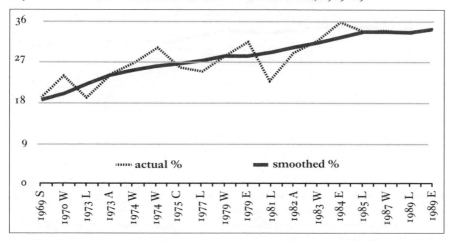

Key: S = Stormont; W = Westminster; L = local government; A = assembly; E = European parliament

Source: B. O'Leary, 'Appendix 4: party support in Northern Ireland, 1969–89' in J. McGarry & B. O'Leary (eds), *The future of Northern Ireland* (Oxford, 1990), pp 342–57.

6.5 Vote share of the Northern nationalist bloc in elections, 1992–2007

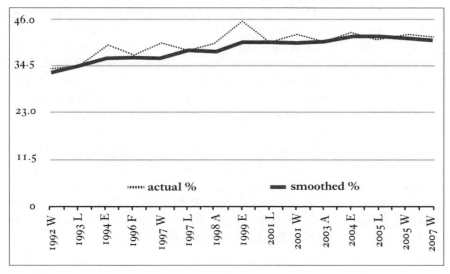

Key: S = Stormont; W = Westminster; L = local government; A = assembly; E = European parliament

Source: Author using data from the Ark website, www.ark.ac.uk/elections.

6.6 Vote share of the Northern nationalist bloc in elections, 2007–16

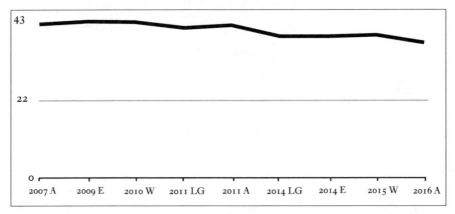

Key: S = Stormont; W = Westminster; L = local government; A = assembly; E = European parliament
Source: Author using data from the Ark website, www.ark.ac.uk/elections.

In the last decade (see figure 6.6) it was debatable whether the Northern nationalist vote displayed trendless fluctuation around a stagnant mean of nearly 40 per cent or was undergoing an actual fall. This is not the place to discuss that subject in depth, but the March 2017 assembly elections suggest a turning point.[20] The DUP's margin of victory over Sinn Féin in March was 0.15 per cent, setting up the prospect of a repeat competition in which Northern nationalists will have strong incentives to switch more of their votes to Sinn Féin. The combined nationalist vote went up to 41.5 per cent, if one counts the People Before Profit Alliance as an all-island party. The combined unionist vote, including the Traditional Unionist Voice (2.6 per cent), the Progressive Unionists (0.7 per cent) and the Conservatives (0.3 per cent), remained a little ahead of the nationalist bloc, at 44.6 per cent. The Others, led by the Alliance Party, took the rest.[21] Northern Ireland therefore has three minorities: nationalists, unionists and others, which partly reflects its new demography (see figure 6.7). The Westminster elections of 2017, under the more primitive electoral system, winner-takes-all in single-member districts, produced a different outcome, but the combined nationalist vote totalled 41.8 per cent (including 0.7 for People Before Profit).

20 Cynics may invoke economist Alex Cairncross' ditty: 'a trend is a trend is trend/the question is will it bend/will it alter its course?/through some unforeseen force/and come to a premature end?' **21** I depend on the draft results here at http://cain.ulst.ac.uk/issues/politics/election/2017nia/ra2017.htm, and round to one decimal place in all cases.

6.7 Religious identifications in the six counties that became Northern Ireland (1861–1911), and in Northern Ireland (1926–2011)

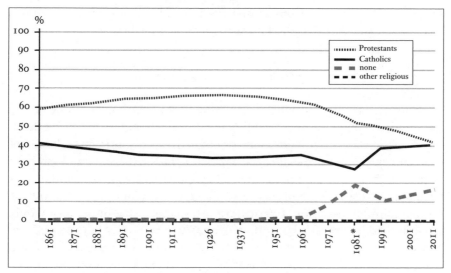

*The 1981 census was subject to a campaign of non-cooperation in some areas, which resulted in a lower-than-expected figure for those stating 'Catholic' and a higher-than-expected figure for 'not stated'. Sources: J. McGarry & B. O'Leary, *Explaining Northern Ireland: broken images* (Oxford, 1995: updated), Census of Ireland and Census of Northern Ireland.

With nationalists and unionists approaching balance, the Others may be pivotal to future developments. That is why UKEXIT matters so much: it has disrupted the initiation of full coexistence since 2007. On remaining within the EU, the Alliance and the Greens, *and* some of the UUP, were fully aligned with Northern nationalists, and 'the European question' will remain an animating source of division until UKEXIT is settled. These developments suggest the possibility of a future alliance among Northern nationalists and most of the Others on most policy questions, ranging from the EU to gay marriage – one that will represent a majority of public opinion in the North, and one that will portray the DUP as the party of a xenophobic and reactionary minority.

Since the negotiations between the embattled Theresa May and the DUP began on 9 June 2017, the DUP has suddenly been receiving greater exposure in Great Britain than that to which it has been accustomed. It has been almost comic to observe the British mass media explaining the party to a largely ignorant electorate. Its corruption questions and its past dalliances with loyalist militias are now daily news and social-media items. The alliance between the Tories and the Ulster unionists in 1911–14 led to the militarization of Irish politics and the Great War, a tragedy; by contrast, the misalliance between the Conservatives and the DUP seems likely to end in a farce, albeit an expensive one for the mass publics of these islands.

SOUTHERN TRANSFORMATIONS

Transformations have also been occurring in the South, albeit quieter and less politically dramatic ones than those in the North. Before reviewing them, one statistic stands out from a census comparison from the first decade of this century. Just 2.1 per cent of the population in Northern Ireland was born in the South, and just 1.3 per cent of the population living in the South was born in the North. Much of this very limited movement occurred across the border counties: a Cork to Carrickfergus trajectory, that of my own family (complicated by my father's work in Africa), was an outlier beyond outliers. These data suggest the remarkable estrangement of the two parts of Ireland that partition reinforced. Movement of people in both directions, at a much higher pace, would signal the openness that would make a consensual reunification easier to accomplish. The point is that it is some distance away; yet, the freedom to move, and at relatively low cost, may be affected by UKEXIT.

The South's recent economic, demographic and cultural transformations should, in principle, have made it a less threatening place to at least some Ulster Protestants. The two decades of high economic growth, 1987–2007, left Ireland's political economy unrecognizable. The first phase, 1987–2002, was one of intensive enrichment, with extensive growth: foreign direct investment-led, with US and EU-related investors to the fore, with high-tech and cutting-edge IT industries and pharmaceuticals prominent in the vanguard, all underpinned by keeping significant public investment in education in hard times. The second phase, 2002–7, however, was marked by unsustainable pseudo-growth, or a bubble, driven by the side-effects of Ireland's membership of the euro, the intoxication of the banking and construction sectors, and severe local regulatory failures, magnified, argued many, by a lax and sometimes corrupt political class.[22] The third phase (2007–17) has been one of austerity, bailouts and, thus far, a recovery, the benefits of which are unevenly spread. UKEXIT has thrown a spanner into

22 See among others D.J. Lynch, *When the luck of the Irish ran out: the world's most resilient country and its struggle to rise again* (New York, 2010); F. O'Toole, *Ship of fools: how stupidity and corruption sank the Celtic Tiger* (New York, 2010).

this recovery, but it is not just a threat; it is also an opportunity. Ireland's growth rate, as Kevin O'Rourke has persuasively argued in his paper, has benefitted from its partial decoupling from the slow-growing UK economy, and from its active participation in the European economy, the largest single market in the world.

Economic forecasting is not yet as good as weather forecasting, but let me nevertheless advance prediction 5: *The new normal argument in estimating the consequences of Irish reunification will suggest that in the longer term Irish unity will be better for both Northern nationalists and Ulster unionists, and of benefit to Ireland as a whole.*[23] In 1921 the Irish Free State's GDP per capita was 45 per cent of what became Northern Ireland, and it used to be said until *c*.2000 that reunification just could not happen because the South could not afford it. In 2012, however, even before Ireland's recovery from the great crash had legs, GDP per capita in Ireland was higher than in the UK, *despite* the great crisis, and *despite* both states' questionable public data (Ireland's tax accounting by multinational corporations (MNCs), and the UK's dubious 'offshore'). Prediction 5 will be boosted in its likelihood if UKEXIT imposes fresh, unexpected costs on Northern Ireland: the UK subvention of the North may fall, or become more contentious if the DUP bids to adjust the Barnett formula; and Northern Ireland's recently won right to have a corporate tax rate that is competitive with that raised by the Dublin government has been rendered pointless if Northern Ireland is to be taken out of the EU, *and* the single market and the customs union. In short, there is now, and has been for some time, a specifically Northern case for Irish unification. Namely, a distinct net per capita benefit for the North from the cumulative benefits of being part of dynamic growth in an Ireland in the single market of the EU. I am not, however, suggesting that this changed economic outlook and discourse will have a significant impact on core unionist support in the North; they are loyal to the crown, not the half-

23 In November 2015 I attended a 'Modeling Irish unification' study at the Harvard Club of New York, presented by Dr Kurt Hüber and Dr Renger Herman van Nieuwkoop. They covered a range of scenarios but suggested that unification potentially could deliver a €35.6 billion boost in GDP for the island in its first eight years, with a more sizable boost in output and incomes in the North, with a 4–7 per cent improvement in GDP; and a more modest boost of between 0.7 to 1.2 per cent in GDP per capita in the Republic. A similar case has been advanced by M. Burke, 'The economic case for Irish unity', pamphlet (2015). I am not competent to endorse or reject these modelling exercises. What I draw to readers' attention is how they reverse the normal presumption that Northern Ireland's status as part of the UK is economically beneficial compared with Irish reunification. What I am predicting in the wake of UKEXIT is that such arguments will become the new normal.

6.8 The extinction of agricultural employment, 1911–2005

Source: Census of Ireland, Census of Northern Ireland.

6.9 The multinationalizing of Ireland

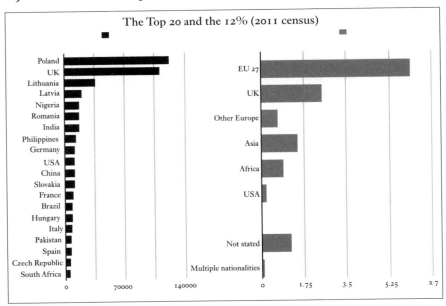

Source: Census of Ireland.

crown; they are British; and I do not insult their preferences or identities by suggesting that they are simply materialists. What may, change, however, are the dispositions of 'the Others', many of whom are of cultural Catholic origin. Moreover, soft Northern nationalists may shift into being more

6.10 The foreign-born in both parts of Ireland: differential Europeanization

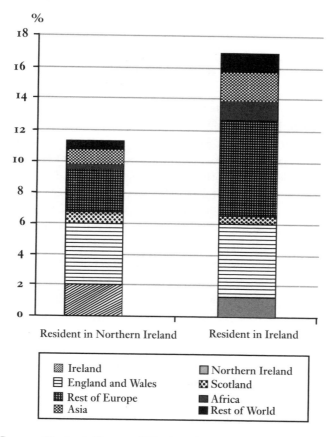

Source: Census of Ireland, Census of Northern Ireland 2011.

enthusiastic unificationists, or, if you prefer, they will favour unification more intensely because it is now in their economic interests, as well as being consonant with their socialization.

Ireland, North and South, is now post-agrarian (see figure 6.8), even if its agribusinesses remain an important part of both economies on the island. Wise policy would seem to require keeping English-speaking independent Ireland attractive for FDI within the EU, and deepening its 'human capital', especially through investing in the research capabilities of universities to increase Ireland's own research and development (R&D), and indigenous exporters. Growth, and the new industries and services, have also had demographic consequences. At the peak of the Celtic Tiger boom Ireland became a land of immigration not migration, boosting its retention and recovery of its native-born population, and attracting multiple new migrants (see figures 6.9 and 6.10). In the first decade of the new millennium Poles and citizens from the EU27 replaced UK citizens as the largest category of foreign-born residents in sovereign Ireland. In short, there was a mild multinationalizing of Ireland. The top twenty countries from which new residents have come are remarkable both for being continental European and global.

Ireland, in short, has become less Irish or more new Irish. Perhaps more importantly, when thinking about Ireland's prospects of becoming a magnet for some liberal Protestants or liberal unionists, is to recognize how much sovereign Ireland has become less Catholic (see figures 6.11 (i) and (ii)). The native-born 'people of the cloth', of all kinds, are fading away. Despite a rising population there are four-fifths less clergy than in 1926. The percentage of Catholics is falling in the South; there has been a revival of Protestantism (also present among new migrants); but it is, however, the de-Catholicization of Catholics that is the most striking phenomenon, and seemingly the most dynamic trend. Census data do not have to be rigorously mined to show that those who identify as atheists or having no religion are correlated with urbanization and places with higher-education institutions – that is, with Ireland's economic and demographic future, not its past. Independent Ireland has access to birth control and divorce. It was the first sovereign state to endorse gay marriage through a referendum, and now among the first to have an openly gay prime minister. It can therefore no longer be described as under Rome's rule on any reasonable construal, even on matters of faith and morals: currently a constitutional convention is considering proposed modifications of the ban on abortion. The point is not that this more diverse, less Catholic, post-Catholic and more ethnically pluralist Ireland will soon win the hearts and minds of hard-line Calvinists, or even less austere Ulster Protestants, to unification. But this secularized Ireland is less threatening to Protestantism, to liberal unionists, and it can be more attractive to the Others in the North – who are both urban and urbane, and disaffected by the white nationalism that has accompanied UKEXIT in England. It is therefore possible that we will witness movement in support for reunification in the North, especially if UKEXIT goes badly for the North. What will matter is whether the Others in the North display volatility on the subject, and whether Northern nationalists can construct durable alliances with liberal unionists.

UKEXIT has already changed estimations of the possibility of unification in the South. Fianna Fáil has been developing a twelve-point plan for a united Ireland – one might suggest that that's not before time for a party that

6.11 (i) Clergy of all religions, excluding students, 1926 and 2006

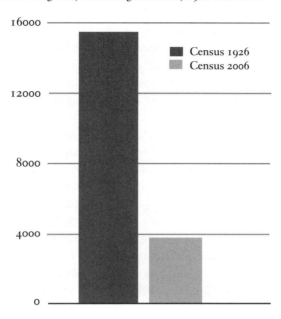

Source: Census of Ireland 1926, Census of Ireland 2006.

6.11 (ii) The rise and partial decline of Catholic Ireland, 1861–2001

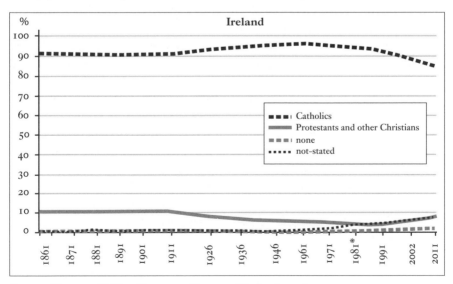

Source: Census of UK, 1861–1911; Census of Ireland, 1926–2011.

was launched in the 1920s. In Philadelphia, the city where I live, in Saint
Patrick's Week 2017, Fine Gael Taoiseach Enda Kenny endorsed the
proposal that Irish citizens across the world, including those in the North,
would have the right in future to vote in Irish presidential elections. Sceptics
wondered whether that was a cunning plan to have a retirement position for
Gerry Adams, but the important point is that the two major parties of the
South now believe they have to have active policies regarding reunification:
that is a big change.

Even considering reunification through referendums, however, at least
under current law and treaties, cannot happen until the Northern Ireland
secretary judges that support for such a possibility is sufficient to justify a
referendum – and that is some way off.[24] It has long been evident that Sinn
Féin cannot achieve unification on its own; for democratic success on
reunification it requires a multi-party alliance, both North and South. A vote
for unification in the North in the immediate future would require a positive
majority vote in the North, not just among Sinn Féin and SDLP voters, but
among the new minorities, and among some liberal unionists. That vista
seems closer than it once did, but as they used to say in Ireland, nearly never
bulled a cow.

PEEKING THROUGH THREE TWILIGHTS

In recent decades there has been discussion of three twilights relevant to our
subject matter. With Geoffrey Evans I have written of the twilight of the
second Protestant ascendancy: unionist dominance, at least as exercised by
Ulster unionist parties within the North, is now over.[25] Dusk, however, never
tells us exactly what the new dawn will look like – and we await considered
loyalist and unionist reaction to the potential loss of the Unionist (with a
capital U) majority in the Northern assembly, and the unfolding of what will
likely be a short-lived Conservative government supported by the DUP.

The second twilight, that of the United Kingdom, was first foretold in
1977 in Tom Nairn's *The break-up of Britain*, a text that merits multiple re-
readings.[26] The jury remains out on this prospect, but prediction 6 cannot be
avoided: *There will be another referendum on Scotland's independence before
there will be a referendum on Irish reunification. The prospect that a majority of
Scots will vote 'yes' will start from a much higher base than in 2014.* The

---

24 http://www.legislation.gov.uk/ukpga/1998/47/schedule/1.   25 B. O'Leary & G.
Evans, 'Northern Ireland: *la fin de siècle*, the twilight of the second Protestant ascendancy
and Sinn Féin's second coming', *Parliamentary Affairs*, 50:4 (1997), 672–80.

breakup of Great Britain is likely to precede the break-up of the union with Northern Ireland because the polls have already shifted in Scotland: the preference for independence runs at between 45 and 50 per cent, before any campaign has begun, and before London experiences any comeuppance in negotiations in Brussels. It is true that in the June 2017 elections the Conservatives and Labour experienced partial recoveries in Scotland, but the SNP remains the dominant party, and will await its moment. The possibility of Scottish independence, as and when that materializes, will leave Ulster unionists rethinking their futures. Ulster unionists have two ethnic homelands of origin, England and Scotland. But what will it mean to be part of the United Kingdom of England, Northern Ireland and Wales (UKENIW is not euphonic), or to be British without Great Britain?

That is among the reasons the expression UKEXIT has been used throughout this paper, rather than BREXIT. The Irish, North and South, though not the Scots, would have less objection if it was just BREXIT that was on the table.[27] In 2009 I co-authored 'Must pluri-national federations fail?'[28] The evidence John McGarry and I reviewed strongly suggests that multinational polities break down because the relevant central government triggers disintegration – usually through unilateral acts of recentralization. The argument is now to be tested to destruction in these islands if the Conservatives, especially a minority Conservative government supported by the DUP, persists on a uniform exit for the entirety of the UK. The cost of UKEXIT may be the break-up of the UK's two unions: the union of Great Britain, and the union of Great Britain with Northern Ireland (that also seems to be the likely order).

The third twilight, that of the gods, is not to repeat the prediction of further secularization – a subject briefly discussed above. Rather the reference is to the bleak prognostications of sociologist Wolfgang Streeck, the last intellectual of stature from the Frankfurt school.[29] He believes that the institutional framework of 'European integration', at least as Germans have imagined it, is experiencing its 'Götterdämmerung'.[30] The end of the EU's 'social dimension' in the 1990s was, he submits, also the end of the EU as a

26 T. Nairn, *The break-up of Britain: crisis and neo-nationalism* (London, 1981). **27** For a longer discussion see B. O'Leary, 'The Dalriada document: towards a multinational compromise that respects democratic diversity in the United Kingdom', *Political Quarterly*, 87:4 (2016), 5618–33. **28** J. McGarry & B. O'Leary, 'Must pluri-national federations fail?' *Ethnopolitics*, 8:1 (2009), 5–26. **29** See W. Streeck, *Buying time: the delayed crisis of Western capitalism* (London, 2013); W. Streeck, 'Why the euro divides Europe', *New Left Review*, 95 (2015); W. Streeck, 'Scenario for a wonderful tomorrow', *London Review of Books*, 38:7 (2016), 7–10. **30** W. Streeck, 'Collapsing constructions: reflections on the British exit' in *The Brexit crisis: a Verso report* (London, 2016), ch. 11.

political body that might protect its populations against neo-liberal restructuring, and re-education or indoctrination. He writes that, 'the constructions have at last begun to crumble, and if their controlled explosion is not begun soon, they will collapse and kill off Europe'.[31] Despite the Wagnerian tone, Streeck is a man of the left, arguing for a return or retreat to the nation-state as the instrument to run each European economy more democratically and fairly. For Streeck, the EU has become a Hayekian prison in which 'the market' is effectively free of democratic control, whence the sound of falling masonry. He does not instruct his readers how to carry out the relevant controlled explosion.

Ironically, Streeck is joined from the right by a true Hayekian, an economic historian from the US, John R. Gillingham. The recent author of nothing less than *The EU: an obituary*,[32] Gillingham refuses the good custom of not publishing an obituary before the relevant entity has ceased to be. He declares that he would prefer a 're-nationalized' Continent, knit together 'through a network of purpose-based, practical, and results-oriented bilateral and multilateral agreements'. We may reasonably ask both Gillingham and Streeck: how exactly would achieving that goal be better, or easier, than having (and reforming) the EU? Gillingham asserts that political and economic cooperation would survive the death of the EU, but does not estimate the probabilities, or provide a plausible path to get there.

From the comfort of a lifetime tenured chair in the US (a position I share), Gillingham urges Europeans to embrace even greater risks than the contracts their member states once made with finance capitalists in the 1990s and 2000s. Exactly why they should follow this counsel is unclear. He insists that:

> The refugee crisis is … only one of several widening, lengthening, and now crisscrossing fissures – many of them caused by Brussels itself – responsible for the crumbling of the EU. The European Depression is the greatest of them. It cannot be ended unless the single currency project is abandoned. In addition, the present monetary regime must be replaced by partly restored national monies, and fiscal independence returned to the nations of Europe. Until this happens, antagonism between North and South, and (increasingly) East and West, as well as across classes and generations, can only mount. This in the end will fuel public anger with, and resentment of, Brussels. While it may take

31 W. Streeck, 'Collapsing constructions: reflections on British exit' in Verso, *The Brexit crisis: a Verso report* (Kindle Locations 829–30; 863–4; 901–2).   32 Published by Verso, the outlet of the British New Left, in 2016.

divergent forms of expression from country to country, the EU will be the final target of this universal ire. The European idea has turned rancid.

Perhaps Gillingham may be right, but I strongly suspect not. Reports of the death of the EU seem premature, even if there is little room for complacency. The EU, including the euro, can be reformed – though there is a need for greater speed and resolution in reforming both, and, personally, I would argue that both need to be made more social, social democratic, and indeed socialist, even if these labels are not necessary: why, for example, can't its central bank be given a mandate that includes full employment, not just price stability, as has been the case in the US for over a century? More prosaically, the UKEXIT negotiations may increase the solidarity of the rest of the EU: the moment provides member states with a strong incentive to ensure that life outside the EU is not better than life within. There is 'strong and stable leadership' ahead – but it is in the EU27, and the EU institutions, in which Ireland is embedded. There will be no bespoke deal for May, or for her successor. Guy Verhofstadt, the European parliament's chief coordinator on UKEXIT, said of the British position that he had previously thought that 'surrealism was a Belgian invention'. The joke is yet to be understood in London. Prediction 7 follows with less but still robust confidence: *There will be no short- or medium-term collapse of the EU in the face of the crises posed by UKEXIT, the management of the euro, the migrant and refugee crises, or the crises in Ukraine and Turkey.* There are further detailed implications of this prediction that cannot be elaborated in the space available, though I made some of them at our conference, e.g., Marine Le Pen will not become the next president of France, and the Alternative for Germany will not be able to displace the German grand coalition, and so on. There has to be a limit to electoral crystal-ball gazing! The suggestion, however, is that populism may have peaked in democratic Europe, with the possible exceptions of Italy and Hungary. The corollary is that it will be the UK, rather than the rest of the EU, that experiences the more painful adjustments from UKEXIT, and if that happens then Northern Ireland is unlikely to be fully protected from such costs unless it is saved by Ireland and the DUP's pursuit of their respective rational interests.

The EU doubtless has to become more redistributive, to compensate those who suffer from market forces (what today goes by the name of globalization), or else it has to retreat, and allow its member states to use social-welfare measures, basic-income polices and debt policies that will partially work against so-called market freedoms. Karl Polanyi's story of how states and societies periodically rebel and re-subordinate markets offers one guide to such a reshaped European future.[33] But that speculation to one side, prediction 8 seems a safe wager: *Ireland's political class, led by Fine Gael, Fianna Fáil and Sinn Féin, the right, centre and left of its reconfigured party system, will remain strongly committed to the EU at least for the next decade, though not to strongly Euro-federalist positions.* Despite the recent painful Euro-austerity measures in Ireland, overseen by the troika, and despite their debatable legitimacy, it remains widely agreed that European institutions have been to Ireland's net benefit, and explain Ireland's attraction to external investors. Former Taoiseach Garret FitzGerald and economic historian Kevin O'Rourke, at separate times, have independently argued that Ireland's European path has justified Ireland's attainment of national sovereignty: the Easter Rising and the war of independence were fully vindicated once dependency on the UK economy was radically reduced. For this reason, among others, Ireland's political class will be deeply reluctant to join British politicians in their latest postcolonial adventure.

By contrast, prediction 9, is, dare I say it, very predictable: *Northern Ireland's political class will remain divided on exit from the EU.* If full UKEXIT happens, and Northern Ireland is not only taken out of the EU, but also the single market and the customs union, then I suspect the evidence will soon demonstrate net harm to the Northern economy – in higher import costs, higher inflation, loss of EU programme-funding, and general UK policy and fiscal restructuring. Such a scenario would damage the DUP and enhance the intensity of the demand for a referendum on unification, especially if the Scots depart the UK. This vista, that Northern Ireland will be dragged out of the EU *and* the single market and the European customs union, against its democratic will as expressed in the June 2016 referendum, and that of all the major parties in North, except the DUP, would seem to be the safe prediction, but I am reluctant to make it.

Unlike Scotland, Northern Ireland has two guardians of its interests. And, if the Northern assembly is suspended – and that would be another breach of the Good Friday Agreement – then the British-Irish Intergovernmental Conference recovers its importance, including the Irish government's right to be consulted on all aspects of public policy affecting the North, an unwelcome prospect for the DUP. In the period ahead Dublin has to facilitate the resolution of three issues before the Northern executive is reformed: whether Arlene Foster will step aside during an official inquiry;

---

33 K. Polanyi, *The great transformation: the political and economic origins of our time* (Boston, 2001 (1944)). See also a useful recent biography by G. Dale, *Karl Polanyi: a life on the left* (New York, 2016).

conflict-legacy questions; and the consequences of UKEXIT. The latter is the fundamental subject that will affect people's futures. One matter is quickly soluble: Dublin will likely at some juncture publicly ask the London government to affirm its commitments to the European Convention on Human Rights in the Good Friday Agreement – if the UK does not oblige then that will hardly advance goodwill for the UK in the UKEXIT negotiations. Any UK bluff to go for a unilateral exit from the EU without a withdrawal agreement – 'no deal is better than a bad deal' was May's mantra – will shortly be tested by the EU27. Bargaining theory tells us that the party that has most to lose is likely to back down first – but we wait to see how rational these agents are; some do a good job of imitating irrational bargainers; perhaps their public boasts and contradictions are just as foolish as they seem. If negotiations do not break down on the UK's membership dues (€62 billion), then the Irish government is well-placed to extract concessions on behalf of the whole island.

The surreal position the Tories have created for themselves means that they have little choice but to beat a retreat from the positions that May staked out, and lost on in the Westminster elections of 2017, despite increasing her party's vote share. They face a profound legislative and legal quagmire: in European law, the clock ticks automatically toward a hard UKEXIT; negotiations have scarcely begun; they now have neither an agreed position nor a credible leadership; they have passed no important preparatory legislation; they must negotiate every step of the way with the DUP; and they seem to have forgotten that these will be the most public negotiations of all time – how does one have leak-free negotiations when twenty-eight states have their interests at stake? The Tories will have to change strategy amid deeply unpropitious conditions. A further economic downturn may be underway, providing another dose of aversion therapy for UKEXIT. Many voters apparently preferred Jeremy Corbyn's high taxes on the top 5 per cent, and greater public expenditure, to May's pain for the many, grammar schools, and taxes on demented grandparents.

It is clearer what it is in Ireland's interests to prioritize, and the UK will need to listen, not least because it's possible that the post-withdrawal agreement, and conceivably the withdrawal agreement itself, may become what the lawyers call 'mixed', that is, it may trigger treaty-ratification requirements in each member state, and therefore a possible referendum in Ireland. Think about that: long before any referendum on Irish reunification 'the plain people of Ireland' may be asked to vote on some UK-EU27 agreement. Since *Crotty vs. An Taoiseach* (1987), any treaty that affects the sovereign rights of the Irish people, especially an EU treaty, requires a constitutional amendment. The attorney general advises on whether a referendum is necessary, but one who advised that one was unnecessary would likely face a court challenge because the UK's withdrawal from the EU almost certainly alters the British-Irish treaty of 1999 and the Good Friday Agreement, not least because the power of the Irish executive will be affected. No referendum on any such agreement will pass if it is significantly opposed to Irish interests, convenience or pride.

Ireland's national interests include maintaining the right of reunification by joint consent, and the Good Friday Agreement, the recital to which – embedded in the British-Irish Agreement of 1999 – presumed the joint membership of the two sovereign governments in the EU's internally borderless single market. Ireland's convenience demands no return of a land border – whether controlling customs, or migration, or manned by armed police. It requires any customs border between Ireland and the EU to be in the Irish Sea, an administratively feasible and convenient idea, which may be acceptable to some unionists, and quite possibly to a majority in the North.[34] Ireland's pride requires that the UK makes concessions to Ireland.

In short, special status for the North will become the agenda that this Dublin government – or its successor – will have to pursue; otherwise it may fall. Overt special status, I suggest, will likely not be granted in name, but it may come in practice – through a bundle of separate pledges and commitments. The EU27 are aware of the consequences of UKEXIT for Ireland, and the Good Friday Agreement, and will not want to damage the core interests of one of its continuing members. Could there be a long phasing out, British-paid, of beneficial EU programmes in the North, ranging from the common agricultural policy to cross-border funds? Could some of those costs be deducted from the €62 billion exit fee? Could there be a long phase-out of Northern Ireland's membership of the full single market (again, British-paid)? Could there be an EU-endorsed agreement that the EU-UK customs are administered on the British side of the Irish Sea? What exactly might be the links between a deal over Gibraltar and a deal over Northern Ireland?

Any Irish government has to recognize Sinn Féin's role as the leading light of Northern nationalists, so it is worth asking what Sinn Féin will accept. In 2016 the party set out its stall in *The case for the North to achieve designated special status within the EU*, a paper with remarkable parallels to the

---

34 This is not the place to elaborate my scepticism about the idea of e-borders, where I have been educated by Dr Tom Lyne. Successful e-borders presume mutual trust among the states that choose to regulate their borders in this manner, and assume minimal criminal racketeering and smuggling.

government of Scotland's white paper *Scotland's place in Europe*. Many of the demands in *The case* are achievable, with the notable exception of the claim that the North's MEP allotment be added to Ireland's representation in the European parliament. The merits of the demands in *The case* is a conversation worth having in Dublin, Belfast, Brussels and London, because they are the benchmarks of a party capable of playing a decisive role in an Irish referendum ratifying a UK-EU27 agreement, either a mixed agreement as part of the withdrawal agreement, a transitional agreement, or a mixed agreement after the UK has exited, or as a coalition partner in a future Irish government.

It is, I suggest, in the interests of all three major Irish parties, and most of their minor rivals, to argue for the functional equivalent of special status for the North, to reduce the damage to the Good Friday Agreement and to cross-border economic co-operation, and to do so, for the first time, with the support of a majority in Northern Ireland. The Conservatives have so far set their face against all such asymmetrical and differentiated proposals, but they may have to bend, not least if they judge that concessions may have to be made to Scotland – and under Ruth Davidson they now have Scottish Tory MPs who want what they call a 'soft BREXIT' and do not wish their brand to be spoiled by the DUP. Special status for the North is practically identical to demanding that Northern Ireland remains in the EU without representation; so is European Economic Area membership for the North; and so is a long period of phasing out EU programmes and single-market membership for the North. A very creative resolution would be to agree the latter, that is, a longer period of Northern membership of the single market and the customs union, with an important additional agreement: to have two referendums, North and South, at the end of the North's single-market/ EEA membership, to determine whether the two political units wish to reunify; and, if they do, to elect a constitutional convention to discuss the constitution of what would still be a significantly economically integrated space. My last prediction is not as bold as this suggestion. I predict that: *Ireland will in due course seek to negotiate for special status for the North, i.e., longer membership for the North within the single market and the customs union than for Great Britain.* Whether it can succeed I do not know.

EU-related provisions in the Good Friday Agreement and the British–Irish Agreement 1999

GOOD FRIDAY AGREEMENT

ALL: We pledge that we will, in good faith, work to ensure the success of each and every one of the arrangements to be established under this agreement. It is accepted that all of the institutional and constitutional arrangements – an Assembly in Northern Ireland, a North/South Ministerial Council, implementation bodies, a British-Irish Council and a British-Irish Intergovernmental Conference and any amendments to British acts of parliament and the constitution of Ireland – are interlocking and interdependent and that in particular the functioning of the Assembly and the North/South Council are so closely inter-related that the success of each depends on that of the other.

ALL: The power of the sovereign government with jurisdiction there [in Northern Ireland] shall be exercised with rigorous impartiality on behalf of all the people in the diversity of their identities and traditions and shall be founded on the principles of full respect for, and equality of, civil, political, social and cultural rights, of freedom from discrimination for all citizens, and of parity of esteem and of just and equal treatment for the identity, ethos, and aspirations of both communities [a passage which impliedly includes EU political rights].

Strand One: Relations with other institutions:
31. Terms will be agreed between appropriate Assembly representatives and the Government of the United Kingdom to ensure effective co-ordination and input by Ministers to national policymaking, including on EU issues.

Strand Two: North-South Ministerial Council
3. The Council to meet in different formats:
    (iii) in an appropriate format to consider institutional or cross-sectoral matters (including in relation to the EU) and to resolve disagreement.

17. The Council to consider the European Union dimension of relevant matters, including the implementation of EU policies and programmes and proposals under consideration in the EU framework. Arrangements to be made to ensure that the views of the Council are taken into account and represented appropriately at relevant EU meetings.

ANNEX [specifying twelve areas for co-operation and implementation]
8. Relevant EU Programmes such as SPPR, INTERREG, Leader II and their successors.

BRITISH–IRISH AGREEMENT 1999

Wishing to develop still further the unique relationship between their peoples and the close co-operation between their countries as friendly neighbours and as partners in the European Union; ...

Art 2: The two Governments affirm their solemn commitment to support, and where appropriate implement, the provisions of the Multi-Party Agreement

ECHR provisions in the Good Friday Agreement

[Regarding Safeguards]

5. (b) the European Convention on Human Rights (ECHR) and any Bill of Rights for Northern Ireland supplementing it, which neither the Assembly nor public bodies can infringe, together with a Human Rights Commission;

    (c) arrangements to provide that key decisions and legislation are proofed to ensure that they do not infringe the ECHR and any Bill of Rights for Northern Ireland;

[Regarding Operation of the [NI] Assembly]

11. The Assembly may appoint a special Committee to examine and report on whether a measure or proposal for legislation is in conformity with equality requirements, including the ECHR/Bill of Rights.

[Regarding Legislation]

26. The Assembly will have authority to pass primary legislation for Northern Ireland in devolved areas, subject to:

    (a) the ECHR and any Bill of Rights for Northern Ireland supplementing it which, if the courts found to be breached, would render the relevant legislation null and void;

[Regarding UK Legislation under Rights, Safeguards and Equality of Opportunity]

2. The British Government will complete incorporation into Northern Ireland law of the European Convention on Human Rights (ECHR), with direct access to the courts, and remedies for breach of the Convention, including power for the courts to overrule Assembly legislation on grounds of inconsistency.

About the contributors

PHILIP PETTIT was born in Ballygar, Co. Galway, and received his BA and MA from NUI (Maynooth) and his PhD from Queen's University Belfast. He is L.S. Rockefeller University Professor of Politics and Human Values at Princeton, and distinguished university professor of philosophy at the Australian National University. He works mainly in moral and political philosophy and in related foundational issues. His books include *The common mind* (1993), *Republicanism* (1997), *Group Agency* (2011), *On the people's terms* (2012), *Just freedom* (2014), and *The robust demands of the good* (2015). *Common minds: themes from the philosophy of Philip Pettit*, ed. G. Brennan, R. Goodin, F. Jackson and M. Smith, appeared from Oxford University Press in 2007. *Philip Pettit – Five themes from his work*, ed. S. Derpmann and D. Schweikard, appeared from Springer in 2016. He is a fellow of the Australian Academies of Humanities and Social Sciences, the American Academy of Arts and Sciences and the British Academy, and an honorary member of the Royal Irish Academy. He holds an honorary doctorate from the NUI (2000, UCD) and from a number of other universities in Europe and North America. He gave the Tanner Lectures in Human Values at Berkeley in 2015, which are due to be published in 2018 under the title *The birth of ethics*. In June 2017 he was named Companion of the Order of Australia.

R.F. (ROY) FOSTER was born in Waterford and educated in Ireland and the United States. A graduate of Trinity College Dublin, he subsequently became professor of modern British history at Birkbeck College, University of London, and in 1991 the first Carroll Professor of Irish History at Oxford and a fellow of Hertford College, retiring in 2016. He was elected a fellow of the British Academy in 1989, a fellow of the Royal Historical Society in 1986, a fellow of the Royal Society of Literature in 1992, a member of the Academia Europea in 2016, and has received honorary degrees from the University of Aberdeen, Queen's University Belfast, Trinity College Dublin, the National University of Ireland, Queen's University Canada, the University of Edinburgh, and University College Dublin, as well as an honorary fellowship at Birkbeck College, University of London. His books include *Charles Stewart Parnell: the man and his family* (1976); *Lord Randolph Churchill: a political life* (1981); *Modern Ireland, 1600–1972* (1988); *The Oxford illustrated history of Ireland* (1989); *Paddy and Mr Punch: connections in Irish and English history* (1993); *The Irish story: telling tales and making it up in Ireland* (2001), which won the 2003 Christian Gauss Award for Literary Criticism; *W.B. Yeats, a life*, i: *The apprentice mage, 1865–1914* (1997), which won the 1998 James Tait Black Prize for biography; *W.B. Yeats, a life*, ii: *The arch-poet, 1915–1939* (2003); *Luck and the Irish: a brief history of change, 1970–2000* (2007); *Words alone: Yeats and his inheritances* (2011); and *Vivid faces: the revolutionary generation in Ireland, 1890–1922* (2014). He is also a well-known critic and broadcaster.

CLAIR WILLS is Leonard L. Milberg Professor of Irish Letters at the University of Princeton. A scholar of Irish and British literature and culture, with a focus on the twentieth century and issues of historical and political representation, she has written and reviewed for the *Irish Times, Guardian, Times Literary Supplement* and *London Review of Books*. She was one of the editors of *The Field Day anthology of Irish women's writing* (2002). Recent books include the prize-winning *That neutral island: a history of Ireland during the Second World War* (2007); *Dublin 1916: the siege of the GPO* (2009); and *The best are leaving: emigration and post-war Irish culture* (2015), a study of Irish migration to post-war Britain. Her latest book, *Lovers and strangers: an immigrant history of post-war Britain* (2017), is a broader cultural history of post-war Britain, told from the perspective of European and Commonwealth immigrants. She is chair of Princeton University's Fund for Irish Studies series of events and seminars.

KEVIN HJORTSHØJ O'ROURKE is the Chichele Professor of Economic History at the University of Oxford, and a fellow of All Souls College. He is also the research director of the Centre for Economic Policy Research, Europe's most prestigious academic economics research network. He was previously professor of economics at Trinity College Dublin, a lecturer and senior lecturer at University College Dublin, where he is currently a visiting professor, and an assistant professor at Columbia University, New York. He has also taught at Sciences Po, Paris.

Kevin received his PhD in economics at Harvard in 1989, having taken his undergraduate degree in TCD. He is a member of the Royal Irish Academy, and a fellow of the British Academy. He was the first Ireland-based researcher to receive a European Research Council Advanced Investigator Award. He has served in the past as president of the European Historical Economics Society, and as a vice president of the Economic History Association. He is currently serving, inter alia, as a senior editor of *Economic Policy*, as a Trustee of the Cliometric Society, and as a council member of the Royal Economic Society.

Kevin has worked extensively on the history of the international economy. Among his publications are the award-winning *Globalization and history* (co-authored with Jeffrey Williamson); *Power and plenty: trade, war, and the world economy in the second millennium* (co-authored with Ronald Findlay); and the two-volume *Cambridge economic history of modern Europe* (co-edited with Stephen Broadberry).

LOUISE RICHARDSON is vice chancellor of the University of Oxford. She was previously principal and vice chancellor of the University of St Andrews. A native of Ireland, she studied history in Trinity College Dublin before gaining her PhD at Harvard University, where she spent twenty years on the faculty of the Harvard Government Department and served as executive dean of the Radcliffe Institute for Advanced Study. She currently sits on the boards of the Carnegie Corporation of New York, the Booker Prize Foundation and numerous other charities.

A political scientist by training, Professor Richardson is recognized internationally as an expert on terrorism and counter-terrorism. Her publications include *Democracy and counterterrorism: lessons from the past* (2007); *What terrorists want: understanding the enemy: containing the threat* (2006); *The roots of terrorism* (2006); and *When allies differ* (1996). She has written numerous articles on international terrorism, British foreign and defence policy, security institutions and international relations, lectured to public, professional, media and education groups, and served on editorial boards for several journals and presses.

Professor Richardson's awards include the Sumner Prize for work towards the prevention of war and the establishment of universal peace, and honorary doctorates from the universities of Aberdeen and St Andrews in Scotland; Trinity College Dublin and Queen's College Belfast in Ireland; Moscow State Institute of International Relations (MGIMO) in Russia; and the University of the West Indies. She is a member of the American Academy of Arts and Sciences, the American Philosophical Society and the Academy of Social Sciences in the United Kingdom, an honorary member of the Royal Irish Academy and a fellow of the Royal Society of Edinburgh.

BRENDAN O'LEARY is Lauder Professor of Political Science at the University of Pennsylvania. He was formerly professor of government at the London School of Economics, where he also did his PhD. Professor O'Leary is international fellow at the Senator Mitchell Institute at the Queen's University Belfast, a member of the US Council on Foreign Relations, and former senior advisor on power-sharing in the Standby Team of the United Nation's Mediation Support Unit. He advised governments and parties in Northern Ireland during the making of the Good Friday Agreement. In 2017 he was invested as an honorary member of the Royal Irish Academy.

Ireland 1916–2016: The Promise and Challenge of National Sovereignty: Academic Programme

Éire 1916–2016: Dóchas agus Dúshlán na Ceannasachta Náisiúnta: Clár na Comhdhála Acadúla

ACADEMIC CONFERENCE VENUE: BAILEY ALLEN HALL, NUI GALWAY

THURSDAY					
DATE & TIME	SESSION TITLE	CHAIR	PLENARY SPEAKER	PAPER TITLE	RESPONDENTS
Thursday, 10 Nov. 2–2:30pm	Opening Address	Dr Jim Browne, president, NUI Galway	Mr Seán Ó Foghlú, secretary general, of the Department of Education and Skills		
Thursday, 10 Nov. 2:30–3:45pm	European Republicanism: The Past and the Potential	Professor Nicholas Canny, NUI Galway	Professor Philip Pettit, Princeton University	'European republicanism: the past and the potential'	Professor Iseult Honohan, University College Dublin
Thursday, 10 Nov. 7–7:30pm	Address by An Taoiseach Enda Kenny TD	Dr Jim Browne, president, NUI Galway			
Thursday, 10 Nov. 7:30–9:45pm	The Promise of 1916	Professor Mary Daly, president, Royal Irish Academy	Professor Roy Foster, University of Oxford	'The promise of 1916: radicalism, radicalization and resettlement, 1916–2016'	• Professor Anne Dolan, Trinity College Dublin • Professor Anthony McElligott, University of Limerick • Dr Ríóna Ní Fhrighil, NUI Galway • Professor Emmet O'Connor, University of Ulster • Professor Graham Walker, Queen's University Belfast

FRIDAY					
DATE & TIME	**SESSION TITLE**	**CHAIR**	**PLENARY SPEAKER**	**PAPER TITLE**	**RESPONDENTS**
Friday, 11 Nov. 9:30–10:00am	Address by Ms Heather Humphreys TD, minister for arts, heritage, regional, rural and Gaeltacht affairs	Mr John Concannon, director, Ireland 2016 Centenary Programme			
Friday, 11 Nov. 10:00–11:45am	Culture and Identity in a Globalized World	Mr Fintan O'Toole, Irish Times	Professor Clair Wills, Princeton University	'Mothers and other others: representing Ireland beyond borders'	• Professor Claire Connolly, University College Cork • Dr Annie Doona, Dún Laoghaire Institute of Art, Design and Technology • Ms Louise Lowe, ANU Productions • Mr John McAuliffe, University of Manchester
Friday, 11 Nov. 2–3.45pm	Economy, Society and the Well-Being of Citizens	Professor John McHale, NUI Galway	Professor Kevin Hjortshøj O'Rourke, University of Oxford	'Independent Ireland in comparative perspective'	• Professor Alan Barrett, Economic and Social Research Institute • Professor Mary Corcoran, Maynooth University • Mr Anthony Foley, Dublin City University • Dr Eoin O'Leary, University College Cork • Dr Conor Skehan, Dublin Institute of Technology

SATURDAY					
DATE & TIME	**SESSION TITLE**	**CHAIR**	**PLENARY SPEAKER**	**PAPER TITLE**	**RESPONDENTS**
Saturday, 12 Nov. 9:30–11:30am	The Challenges, Promise and Responsibility of Education in the Twenty-First Century	Dr Mary Canning, board member, Higher Education Authority	Professor Louise Richardson, University of Oxford	'The role of education in addressing the challenges of the twenty-first century'	• Professor Dympna Devine, University College Dublin • Professor Willie Donnelly, Waterford Institute of Technology • Dr Niamh Hourigan, University College Cork • Professor Fionnuala Waldron, Dublin City University – St Patrick's Campus
Saturday, 12 Nov. 2–3:30pm	Political Futures and New Paradigms	Dr Maurice Manning, chancellor of the National University of Ireland and chair of the Expert Advisory Group on Commemorations	Professor Brendan O'Leary, Lauder Professor of Political Science at the University of Pennsylvania	'Political futures and new paradigms'	• Dr Niall Ó Dochartaigh, NUI Galway • Professor Jennifer Todd, University College Dublin

Index

Page numbers in bold refer to figures